Beyond Malthus

OTHER NORTON/WORLDWATCH BOOKS

Lester R. Brown et al.

State of the World 1984	*State of the World 1996*
State of the World 1985	*State of the World 1997*
State of the World 1986	*State of the World 1998*
State of the World 1987	*State of the World 1999*
State of the World 1988	*Vital Signs 1992*
State of the World 1989	*Vital Signs 1993*
State of the World 1990	*Vital Signs 1994*
State of the World 1991	*Vital Signs 1995*
State of the World 1992	*Vital Signs 1996*
State of the World 1993	*Vital Signs 1997*
State of the World 1994	*Vital Signs 1998*
State of the World 1995	

ENVIRONMENTAL ALERT SERIES

Lester R. Brown et al.
Saving the Planet

Lester R. Brown
Who Will Feed China?

Alan Thein Durning
How Much Is Enough?

Lester R. Brown
Tough Choices

Sandra Postel
Last Oasis

Michael Renner
Fighting for Survival

Lester R. Brown
Hal Kane
Full House

David Malin Roodman
*The Natural Wealth
of Nations*

Christopher Flavin
Nicholas Lenssen
Power Surge

Chris Bright
Life Out of Bounds

BEYOND MALTHUS

Nineteen Dimensions of the Population Challenge

Lester R. Brown
Gary Gardner
Brian Halweil

The Worldwatch Environmental Alert Series
Linda Starke, Series Editor

W·W· NORTON & COMPANY
New York London

41208588

Worldwatch Database Disk

The data from all graphs and tables contained in this book, as well as from those in all other Worldwatch publications of the past two years, are available on floppy, 3 ¹/₂-inch (high-density) disks for use with IBM-compatible or Macintosh computers. This includes data from the State of the World *and* Vital Signs *series of books,* Worldwatch Papers, World Watch *magazine, and the Environmental Alert series of books. The data (in spreadsheet format) are provided as Microsoft Excel 5.0/95 workbook (*.xls) files. Users must have spreadsheet software installed on their computer that can read Excel workbooks for Windows. To order, send check or money order for $89 plus $4 shipping and handling, or credit card number and expiration date (Mastercard, Visa, or American Express), to Worldwatch Institute, 1776 Massachusetts Ave., NW, Washington DC 20036. Or you may call 1-800-555-2028, fax us at 1-202-296-7365, or reach us by e-mail at wwpub@worldwatch.org.*

Visit our Web site at www.worldwatch.org

The text of this book is composed in Plantin
with the display set in Zapf Book Medium.
Composition by Worldwatch Institute; manufacturing by the Haddon Craftsmen, Inc.

ISBN 0-393-31906-7

W.W. Norton & Company, Inc., 500 Fifth Avenue, New York, N.Y. 10110
http://www.wwnorton.com

W.W. Norton & Company Ltd., 10 Coptic Street, London WC1A 1PU

1 2 3 4 5 6 7 8 9 0

Contents

II. Conclusion   *109*

Acknowledgments

All Worldwatch publications are born of a network of staff members who nurture a project from conceptual infancy to maturity as a manuscript. From brainstorming sessions that spurred insights to administrative efforts that facilitated outreach, this book is no different.

The internal chapters draw heavily on the Institute's on-going research on emerging global issues. Nearly all of the Institute's research staff were consulted for advice on chapters related to their areas of expertise, and to them we are grateful. The water chapter relies on the work of former Worldwatcher Sandra Postel; the biodiversity chapter leans on recent writings of John Tuxill and Chris Bright; Anne Platt McGinn's work on the state of the world's fisheries provided context and background for the chapter on oceanic fish catch and she also offered guidance on the infectious diseases chapter; the materials chapter draws heavily on work by Payal Sampat; Seth Dunn and Christopher Flavin offered advice on the energy and climate change chapters; Ashley Mattoon also provided suggestions on the climate change chapter, and her work with Janet Abramovitz provided a starting point for the forests chapter; Michael Renner's work on conflict and environmental degradation helped to focus the chapter on conflict.

The insightful comments of Hilary French strengthened the entire draft by highlighting our weak points and areas of oversimplification. We appreciate the help of Reah Janise Kauffman for structural suggestions, for coordination of the paper's early drafts, and for enthusiastic support for the concept of the book.

Several external reviewers also provided suggestions on preliminary drafts of individual chapters or the entire manuscript, including Carl Haub, Marilyn Hempel, Kerry MacQuarrie, Karen Stanecki, and Bob Young. Joseph Chamie, Joseph Grinblat, and Thomas Büettner of the United Nations Population Division provided key data, as well as explanations of population projection methods.

We also thank the Worldwatch Communications staff for the work that began once the writing had ended. Dick Bell offered strategic and thoughtful comments, as well as coordinating publishing activities. Mary Caron and Amy Warehime skillfully handled outreach efforts, and Liz Doherty managed the graphics and layout with confidence that calms us all.

And finally, our thanks to Linda Starke, our editor, for her exceptional skill in melding the writing of three authors with three different styles into a coherent whole.

Early financial support for this project came from the David and Lucile Packard Foundation. We would like to applaud their strong and expanding population program. Additional foundation support for research at the Institute comes from the following: the Geraldine R. Dodge Foundation, the Ford Foundation, the William and Flora Hewlett Foundation, the W. Alton Jones Foundation, the John D. and Catherine T. MacArthur Foundation, the Charles Stewart Mott Foundation, the Curtis and Edith Munson Foundation, the Rasmussen Foundation, the Rockefeller Brothers Fund, Rockefeller Financial Services, the Summit Foundation, the Surdna Foundation, the Turner Foundation, the U.N. Population Fund, the Wallace Genetic Foundation, the Wallace Global Fund, the Weeden Foundation, and the Winslow Foundation. We are also grateful for the generosity of the numerous individuals in the Friends of Worldwatch campaign. Special appreciation goes to the Council of Sponsors: Tom and Cathy Crain, Toshishige Kurosawa, Kazuhiko Nishi, Roger and Vicki Sant, Robert Wallace, and Eckert Wintzen.

Finally, we would like to dedicate this book to Bella Abzug and Sidonie Chiapetta, two inspirational members of the population community who passed away this year. For their tireless efforts to advance the status of women, strengthen family planning programs, and promote basic human rights, the world is indebted.

Lester R. Brown, Gary Gardner,
and Brian Halweil

Foreword

This book is an expansion of a Worldwatch Paper entitled *Beyond Malthus: Sixteen Dimensions of the Population Problem*, which was published in September 1998. There are several reasons for expanding the Paper into a short book. One, sales of the Paper have been exceptionally strong, indicating a keen worldwide interest in an interdisciplinary analysis of the population issue. Two, at book length, we can comfortably include additional information that could not be included in a monograph-length publication, including three additional dimensions. And three, by publishing the analysis in book length, we make it available to our worldwide network of book publishers in some 30 languages.

When we started the project, we envisaged a sort of

demographic *Vital Signs,* a shorter version of our annual book that typically contains analyses of some 50 of
the key trends that are shaping our future. Our intent
here was simply to look at various indicators, such as
the oceanic fish catch, carbon emissions, or housing,
through a "per capita lens." We planned to present and
analyze each of the 16 indicators and then add a brief
overview, but as the analysis unfolded we began to see
something that we had not noticed before—the emergence of what we came to call "demographic fatigue"
in many countries.

In countries that have experienced rapid population
growth for several decades, the challenge of simultaneously educating ever growing numbers of youngsters,
of finding jobs for all those entering the labor market,
and of coping with the various environmental consequences of rapid population growth is clearly overwhelming them. When new threats arise, such as AIDS
or aquifer depletion, governments simply cannot cope.

For example, whereas industrial countries have
been able to hold HIV infection rates under 1 percent
of their adult populations, in several countries in sub-
Saharan Africa these have soared to 20–26 percent.
Without a dramatic medical breakthrough in the near
term, these countries will lose one fifth to one fourth of
their adult populations within the next decade. This, we
quickly saw, would dramatically alter existing population projections. Some countries where populations
were projected to double or triple over the next half-
century would in fact have declining numbers in the
short term. In this analysis, as the *Washington Post*
noted, we anticipated the lowering of population projections released by the United Nations in late October.

Another reason for wanting to expand this monograph into a book was our sense that the HIV epidemic was being grossly underestimated. Unless a low-cost cure is developed soon for those living in low-income developing countries, this epidemic will take a massive toll on human life. To find a historical precedent, we had to go back to the sixteenth-century smallpox epidemic that resulted from the introduction of smallpox into New World Indian populations by Europeans, and before that, to the introduction of the bubonic plague into Europe from Central Asia in the fourteenth century. The shocking reality is that, if the HIV epidemic continues unchecked for even a few more years, it could claim more lives in the early twenty-first century than World War II did during this one.

We also decided to issue a book on population now because of three important milestones in 1999. First, this year is the fifth anniversary of the 1994 Cairo conference on population and development, which will provide the occasion for another U.N. conference: Cairo+5. Second, in August 1999, the population in India is expected to pass the 1 billion mark, at which point it will join China in an unenviable 1 billion club. And third, according to the latest calculations by U.N. demographers, the world will pass the 6 billion mark on 12 October 1999. This means the infant that takes us beyond 6 billion will have been conceived by mid-January 1999.

A few weeks after we published the Worldwatch Paper and just days before the United Nations released the new population projections, the congressional leadership in Washington deleted funding for the U.N. Population Fund, the principal source of international family planning assistance and, as such, a key bulwark in halting the spread of the HIV virus. One purpose of this book is to help people everywhere realize that the condoms that help limit population growth also help to limit the spread of HIV.

One final point of clarification. In the Worldwatch Paper we used the 1996 U.N. population projections. In this book we use the late 1998 update, which incorporates new data on fertility trends and, for the first time, the effects of AIDS on mortality. U.N. demographers have not yet had time, however, to include the effect of AIDS on fertility—principally the effect on future population growth of high AIDS mortality rates among young women of reproductive age. When this is done, population projections will be lowered further. The 1998 projection of global population in 2050 of 8.9 billion is down nearly 500 million from the 1996 projection of 9.4 billion, partly because of lower fertility and partly because of the higher mortality from AIDS. The lower projections do not alter the overall analysis found in the Worldwatch Paper.

We welcome comments on this analysis and suggestions for future research topics. We also invite you to visit our Web site at <www.worldwatch.org> for additional information on the topics covered in this book.

Lester R. Brown
Gary Gardner
Brian Halweil

Worldwatch Institute
1776 Massachusetts Ave., N.W.
Washington, D.C. 20036

January 1999

Beyond Malthus

1

The Population Challenge

During the last half-century, world population has more than doubled, climbing from 2.5 billion in 1950 to 5.9 billion in 1998. Those of us born before 1950 are members of the first generation to witness a doubling of world population. Stated otherwise, there has been more growth in population since 1950 than during the 4 million preceding years since our early ancestors first stood upright.[1]

This unprecedented surge in population, combined with rising individual consumption, is pushing our claims on the planet beyond its natural limits. Water tables are falling on every continent as demand exceeds the sustainable yield of aquifers. Our growing appetite for seafood has taken oceanic fisheries to their limits and beyond. Collapsing fisheries tell us we can go no further.

The Earth's temperature is rising, promising changes in climate that we cannot even anticipate. And we have inadvertently launched the greatest extinction of plant and animal species since the dinosaurs disappeared.

Great as the population growth of the last half-century has been, it is far from over. U.N. demographers project an increase over the next half-century of another 2.8 billion people, somewhat fewer than the 3.6 billion added during the half-century now ending. In contrast to the last 50 years, however, all of the 2.8 billion will be added in the developing world, much of which is already densely populated.

Even as we anticipate huge further increases in population, encouraging demographic news seems to surface regularly. Fertility rates, the average number of children born to a woman, have fallen steadily in most countries in recent decades. Twice in the last 10 years the United Nations has moderated its projections of global population growth, first in 1996 and then again in 1998. Unfortunately, part of the latter decline in population projections is due to rising mortality rather than declining fertility.[2]

In contrast to the projected doublings and triplings for some developing countries, populations are stable or even declining in some 32 industrial nations. Compared with the situation at mid-century, when nearly all signs pointed to galloping population increases for the foreseeable future, today's demographic picture is decidedly more complex.

Anyone tempted to conclude that population growth is becoming a "non-issue" may find this book a reality check. Despite the many encouraging demographic trends, the need to stabilize global population is as urgent as ever. Although the rate of population growth is slowing, the world is still adding some 80 million people per year. And the number of young people coming of reproductive age—those between 15 and 24 years old—will be far larger during the early part of the next century than ever before. Through their reproductive choices, this group will heavily influence whether population is stabilized sooner rather than later, and with less rather than more suffering.[3]

In addition, population growth has already surpassed sustainable limits on a number of environmental fronts. From cropland and water availability to climate change and unemployment, population growth exacerbates existing problems, making them more difficult to manage. The intersection of the arrival of a series of environmental limits and a potentially huge expansion in the number of people subject to those limits makes the turn of the century a unique time in world demographic history.

★   ★   ★   ★

The rate of global population growth has been slowing since the 1960s, when birth rates began to decline in many countries as a result of changing cultural, religious, and socioeconomic cues. As families moved to cities, large numbers of children were no longer needed as agricultural laborers; they became instead an economic burden for families. The increasing reach of radio and television altered the aspirations of billions of people, while rising school enrollment and economic progress exposed young men and women to opportunities beyond family life. Meanwhile, the growing acceptance and availability of family planning afforded couples a viable means to reduce the number of children they chose to have. Taken together, these trends helped lower the growth rate of world population from its peak rate of 2.2 percent in 1963 to 1.3 percent in 1998.[4]

Although still an issue of global importance, population growth carries greater urgency in some countries than in others. In contrast to mid-century, when populations were growing everywhere, growth rates now vary more widely across countries than at any time in history. Some countries have stabilized their populations while others are expanding at 3 percent or more per year—a rate that yields a 20-fold increase within a century.

Some 32 countries, with 12 percent of the world's people, have essentially achieved population stability, with growth rates below 0.4 percent per year. With the exception of Japan, all 32 are in Europe, and all are industrial countries. Some of these, including Russia, Japan, and Germany, are actually projected to see population declines over the next half-century.[5]

In another group of 39 countries, fertility has dropped to replacement level—roughly two children per couple—but populations will continue to grow for several decades because a disproportionately large number of young people are moving into the reproductive age group. Among the countries in this category are China and the United States, the world's first and third largest countries, which together contain 26 percent of the world's people.[6]

At the other end of the spectrum, the high-growth end, seven countries are projected to triple their populations before they stabilize. Another group—59 countries, mostly in Africa—is set to double and in some cases nearly triple their populations by 2050. A third group of developing countries, also 59 in number, fall short of a doubling in the next half-century, though they are still far from population stability.

Among the more rapidly growing countries are three large ones facing enormous increases in population in coming decades. (See Table 1–1.) Ethiopia's current population of 58 million is projected to nearly triple, as

TABLE 1–1. *The 20 Largest Countries Ranked According to Population Size, 1998, With Projections to 2050*

	1998		2050	
Rank	Country	Population (million)	Country	Population (million)
1	China	1,243	India	1,529
2	India	989	China	1,478
3	United States	270	United States	349
4	Indonesia	207	Pakistan	345
5	Brazil	162	Indonesia	312
6	Russia	147	Brazil	244
7	Pakistan	142	Nigeria	244
8	Japan	126	Bangladesh	212
9	Bangladesh	123	Ethiopia	169
10	Nigeria	122	The Congo	160
11	Mexico	98	Mexico	147
12	Germany	82	Philippines	131
13	Viet Nam	79	Viet Nam	127
14	Philippines	75	Russia	121
15	Egypt	66	Egypt	115
16	Turkey	65	Iran	115
17	Iran	64	Japan	105
18	Thailand	61	Turkey	101
19	France	59	Tanzania	81
20	Ethiopia	58	Thailand	74

SOURCE: Population Reference Bureau, "1998 World Population Data Sheet," wall chart (Washington, DC: June 1998); United Nations, *World Population Prospects: The 1998 Revision* (New York: December 1998).

it climbs to 169 million in 2050. Pakistan's population is projected to go from 142 million to 345 million, nearly surpassing that of the United States. Nigeria, meanwhile, is projected to go from 122 million today to 244 million, giving it slightly more people in 2050 than there were in all of Africa in 1950. Given the environmental constraints already facing these countries, especially the growing scarcity of water and cropland, it is unlikely that their projected population increases will actually materialize. The question is whether lower than projected growth will be realized because of societal choices to moderate growth, or because nature ruthlessly imposes its own constraints.

Although the rate of world population growth is slowing, far more people are now added to the planet each year—some 80 million—than in 1963, when the growth rate crested. This is because of the momentum inherent in population growth, a momentum that requires decades to exhaust. This illustrates the importance of early action to stabilize population. It also suggests why the reproductive choices of the generation now entering adulthood are so important: the consequences of their choices will be felt for decades to come.

★   ★   ★   ★

As the global population locomotive hurtles forward—despite pressure applied to the demographic brakes—there are hazards on the tracks ahead. A number of limits to sustainability are being surpassed, or are about to be. This book looks at the consequences of population growth for 19 environmental and social dimensions of the human experience, and concludes that any number of imminent hazards could trigger a demographic train wreck.

In this respect, we are part of a long tradition dating back to 1798 when Thomas Malthus, a British clergyman and intellectual, warned in his "Essay on the Principle of Population" of the check on population growth provided by what he believed were coming constraints on food supplies. Noting that population grows exponentially while food supply grows only arithmetically, Malthus foresaw massive food shortages and famine as an inevitable consequence of population growth.[7]

Critics of Malthus point out that his pessimistic scenario never unfolded. His supporters believe he was simply ahead of his time. On the bicentennial of Malthus' legendary essay, and in an era of environmental decline, we find his focus on the connection between resource supply and population growth to be particularly useful. We move beyond Malthus's focus on food, however, to look at several resources—such as water and forests—whose supply may be insufficient to support projected increases in population. We also examine social phenomena including disease and education, and analyze the effect of population growth on these.

The results of our analysis offer further evidence that we are approaching—and increasingly broaching—any number of natural limits. We know that close to a tenth of world food production relies on the overpumping of groundwater, and that continuing this practice will mean a substantial decline in food production at some point in the future. We know that both atmospheric carbon dioxide concentrations and the Earth's surface temperature are rising. We know that we are the first species in the planet's history to trigger a mass extinction, and we admit that we do not understand the consequences of such a heavy loss of plant and animal species. In short, we know enough to understand that the growth in our numbers and the scale of our activities is already redirecting the natural course of our planet, and that this new direction will in turn affect us.

The relationship between these natural limits and population growth becomes clear if we contrast key trends projected for the next half-century with those of the last one. For example, since 1950 we have seen a near fivefold growth in the oceanic fish catch and a doubling in the supply of fish per person, but people born today may well see the catch per person cut in half as population grows during their lifetimes. Marine biologists now believe we may have "hit the wall" in oceanic fisheries and that the oceans cannot sustain a catch any larger than today's.[8]

Similarly, the finite area that can be cultivated for grain is a worrisome natural limit as population increases. Grainland per person has been shrinking since mid-century, but the drop projected for the next 50 years means the world will have less grainland per person than India has today. Future population growth is likely to reduce this key number in many societies to the point where they will no longer be able to feed themselves. Countries such as Ethiopia, India, Iran, Nigeria, and Pakistan will see grainland per person shrink by 2050 to less than one tenth of a hectare (one fourth of an acre)—far smaller than a typical suburban building lot in the United States.[9]

Meanwhile, with the amount of fresh water produced each year essentially fixed by nature, population growth shrinks the water available per person and results in severe shortages in some areas. Countries now experiencing this include China and India, as well as scores of smaller ones. As irrigation water is diverted to industrial and residential uses, the resultant water shortages could drop food production per person in many countries below the survival level.

The fast-deteriorating water situation in India was described in July 1998 in one of India's leading newspapers, the *Hindustan Times*: "If our population continues to grow as it is now...it is certain that a major part of the country would be in the grip of a severe water famine in 10 to 15 years." The article goes on to reflect an emerging sense of desperation. "Only a bitter dose of compulsory family planning can save the coming generation from the fast-approaching Malthusian catastrophe." Among other things, this comment appears to implicitly recognize the emerging conflict between the reproductive rights of the current generation and the survival rights of the next generation.[10]

As difficult as it is to imagine the addition of another 2.8 billion people to the world's population, it is even harder to grasp the effects of the rising affluence of a growing population. As we look back over the last half-century, we see that world fuelwood use doubled, paper use increased nearly sixfold, grain consumption nearly tripled, water use tripled, and fossil fuel burning increased some fourfold.[11]

The relative contribution of population growth and rising affluence to the growth in demand for various resources varies widely. With fuelwood use, most of the doubled use is accounted for by population growth. With paper, in contrast, rising affluence is primarily responsible for the growth in use. For grain, population accounts for most of the growth, since consumption per person has risen only 30 percent since 1950. Similarly with water. For fossil fuels, the growth in use is rather evenly divided between population growth and rising consumption.

Any meaningful assessment of the future pressures on resources must take into account both population growth and rises in affluence. Consumption per person of various resources among societies can vary from 5 to 1 for grain, as between the United States and India, for example, to easily 20 to 1 for energy. While population growth in some 32 countries has stabilized, and many more countries have stabilization as a goal, no country at any level of affluence has announced or even seriously contemplated limits on consumption per person.[12]

In this book, the focus is on population growth as a variable. For those interested in an analysis of the effect of rising affluence on the Earth's resources, we recommend an earlier Worldwatch/Norton book in this series, *How Much is Enough?*, by Alan Durning.

The challenge to nations presented by continuing rapid population growth is not limited to natural resources. It also includes social and economic needs, including education, housing, and jobs. During the last half-century, the world has fallen further and further behind in creating jobs, leading to record levels of unemployment and underemployment. Unfortunately, over the next 50 years the number of entrants into the job market will be even greater, pushing the ranks of unemployment to levels that could be politically destabilizing. And as homelessness is already a serious problem in most large Third World cities, the housing situation for additional urban dwellers is increasingly dismal.

The Earth is more crowded today than ever before. And although our numbers continue to grow, the size of the planet on which we live remains the same. Future population growth has the potential to further degrade and deplete resources, such as topsoil, groundwater, and forest cover, as well as to reduce the resources available to each person. Moreover, population growth strains the capacity of governments to provide basic social services, such as education and health care, for each citizen. This combination of environmental degradation and social shortfalls can ultimately result in any number of unpleasant scenarios that can undermine future progress.

★   ★   ★   ★

Our analysis of the population challenge uses the medium U.N. population projection released in December 1998, which shows world population expanding from 6.1 billion in 2000 to 8.9 billion in 2050, a gain of 2.8 billion. While this is judged by U.N. demographers as the scenario "most likely" to materialize, it is by no means an inevitable development for the next century for two reasons. First, the U.N. projections do not take into account possible environmental or social constraints on population expansion. And second, couples worldwide may choose to have fewer children than the U.N. projections assume. In summary, the U.N. projections do not account for the possibility of human actions—both intended and unintended—to alter our demographic destiny.

The U.N.'s projections are mainly demographic, based on historical data on fertility, mortality, and average life span and on the likely course of current social and political phenomena such as refugee movements, wars, and the spread of AIDS. No effort was made, however, to incorporate factors affecting national carrying capacities, such as the adequacy of water supplies or cropland. Indeed, because the projections are based exclusively on demographic assumptions and do not take into account the environmental and social limits to carrying capacity, they should be viewed as a first pass rather than the final word on estimates of future population.

In this sense, the projections may be misleading, because they give the impression that projected population increases are likely, when in reality ecological and social life-support systems may collapse long before they can materialize. To cite a single example: Yemen's projected growth during the next 50 years from 18 million to 59 million seems unlikely for the desert nation, which already has only 0.03 hectares of grainland per person and faces severe water shortages and dismal socioeconomic indicators.[13]

The 19 dimensions analyzed in this book help to put the U.N. numbers in perspective by sketching some of the parameters—ranging from disease and conflict outbreaks to food and water shortages—that could reduce population growth in some countries below the levels projected. By raising mortality levels, these constraints can drive down the very population growth rates that first bred the constraints. We consider some of these possible feedback loops in Chapter 21, where we assess the feasibility of the U.N. projections and discuss "demographic fatigue"—the growing inability of poor governments with burgeoning populations to cope with new threats to society.

A more hopeful path is for population growth to be stabilized by intelligent and humane economic and social policies. In addition to the medium-level projection, the U.N. offered two alternatives, which differ from the most likely projection in how many children couples worldwide eventually decide to bear (and how quickly they get there). As of 1998, the world average stood at roughly 2.7 children per couple. The high-level projection, which assumes that couples will eventually settle at 2.6 children, puts population at 10.7 billion by 2050; the medium-level projection used throughout this book assumes that couples will have on average 2.1 children, with population reaching 8.9 billion by 2050; the low-level projection, which assumes that couples will end up having 1.6 children, puts population at 7.3 billion by 2050.[14]

Though this low-level trajectory may seem rather optimistic, most demographers agree that fertility declines faster today than in the past. The socioeconomic, political, and cultural landscape that influences fertility levels now shifts rapidly, so that the transition to low fertility levels occurs quickly. Over the last few decades, demographers have been surprised again and again by the rapid decline in the number of children couples choose to bear throughout the world. Even as recently as a decade ago, demographers would have been hesitant to project that fertility rates would be as low as they are today in many developing countries.[15]

Nonetheless, the transition to lower fertility levels cannot be taken for granted. Settling at the lower population trajectory depends on a renewed commitment from the international community to maintain the dominant global trend toward fewer children per couple. In Chapter 21 we discuss the changes in policy that all nations—especially those where population is still growing rapidly—will need to adopt to further slow population growth.

Several questions stand out in trying to look beyond Malthus. Will countries with rapid population growth take control of their reproductive destinies and quickly shift to smaller families? Or will they fail to do so, and instead watch the resulting spread of disease, hunger, or social disintegration lead to rising death rates? In a world facing many problems as it prepares to enter the next century, stabilizing population may be the most difficult challenge of all.

I

Population Growth and ...

2

Grain Production

The relationship between the growth in world population and the grain harvest has shifted over the last half-century, neatly dividing this period into two distinct eras. From 1950 to 1984, growth in the grain harvest easily exceeded that of population, raising the harvest per person from 247 kilograms to 342, a gain of 38 percent. (See Figure 2–1.) During the 14 years since then, growth in the grain harvest has fallen behind that of population, dropping output per person from its historic high in 1984 to an estimated 312 kilograms in 1998—a decline of 9 percent, or 0.7 percent a year.[1]

These global trends conceal widely divergent developments among countries, contrasts that can be seen for the world's two most populous ones: India and China. In both, grain production per person was close

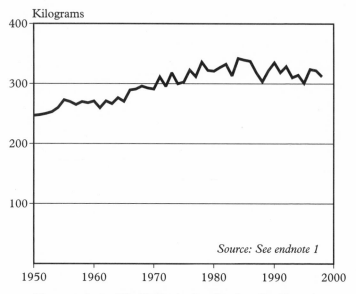

FIGURE 2–1. *World Grain Production Per Person,*
1950–98

to 200 kilograms as recently as 1978. Since then, the
figure in India has edged up slightly but still falls short
of 200 kilograms, while in China production has
surged since the economic reforms in 1978, with output per person now at nearly 300 kilograms. The combination of a dramatic surge in grain production and an
equally dramatic reduction in population growth has
given China a large margin of safety, effectively eliminating most of its hunger and malnutrition. Meanwhile, although India has also achieved impressive
gains in its harvest, these have been largely canceled
by population growth, leaving most of its 989 million
people living close to the margin.[2]

What has happened in China and India is the story
of developing countries in general. The overwhelming

majority have achieved substantial, if not dramatic, gains in their grain harvests over the last half-century. Some, such as Thailand, have combined this with a much slower growth of population, which means that agricultural gains translate into rising grain production per person. In Pakistan, by contrast, grain production per person climbed steadily for awhile, but it peaked in 1981 at 186 kilograms. Since then it has been declining nearly 1 percent a year. In effect, Pakistan's farmers are losing the battle with population growth.[3]

The slower growth in the world grain harvest since 1984 is due to the lack of new land and to slower growth in irrigation and fertilizer use. Irrigated area per person, after expanding by 29 percent from 1950 until 1978, has declined by 4 percent since then as growth in the irrigated area has fallen behind that of population.[4]

The increase in world fertilizer use has slowed dramatically since 1990, as diminishing returns to the application of additional fertilizer have stabilized use in the United States, Western Europe, and Japan and slowed annual growth in world fertilizer use from 6 percent between 1950 and 1990 to scarcely 2 percent in recent years.[5]

Although Malthus was primarily concerned with the additional demand for grain generated by population growth, rising affluence is also playing a role. In a low-income country such as India, grain consumption per person is less than 200 kilograms per year and diets are typically dominated by a single starchy staple—rice, for instance. With scarcely a pound of grain available a day per person, nearly all must be consumed directly, leaving little for conversion into animal protein. For the average American, on the other hand, the great bulk of the 900-kilogram yearly grain consumption is taken in indirectly in the form of beef, pork, poultry, eggs, milk, cheese, ice cream, and yogurt. At the intermediate level, in a country like Italy, people consume roughly 400 kilograms of grain a year.[6]

One question often asked is, How many people can the Earth support? This must be answered with another question, At what level of consumption? If the world grain harvest of 1.85 billion tons were expanded to 2 billion tons in the years ahead, it would support 10 billion Indians or 2.2 billion Americans. To answer the question of how many people the Earth can support, we first have to know the level of consumption we expect to live at. The bottom line is that future food price stability depends on expanding production fast enough to keep up with both population growth and rising affluence.[7]

Now that the frontiers of agricultural settlement have disappeared, future growth in grain production must come almost entirely from raising land productivity. Unfortunately, this is becoming more difficult. After rising at 2.1 percent a year from 1950 to 1990, the annual increase in grainland productivity dropped to scarcely 1 percent from 1990 to 1997. The challenge for the world's farmers is to reverse this decline at a time when cropland area per person is shrinking, the amount of irrigation water per person is dropping, and the crop yield response to additional fertilizer use is falling.[8]

3

Fresh Water

Wherever population is growing, the supply of fresh water per person is declining. As a result of population growth, the amount of water available per person from the hydrological cycle will fall by 73 percent between 1950 and 2050. Stated otherwise, there will be scarcely one fourth as much fresh water per person in 2050 as there was in 1950. With water availability per person projected to decline dramatically in many countries already facing shortages, the full social effects of future water scarcity are difficult even to imagine. Indeed, spreading water scarcity may be the most underrated resource issue in the world today.[1]

Evidence of water stress can be seen as rivers are drained dry and as water tables fall. The Colorado River in the southwestern United States now rarely reaches the sea. The Yellow River, the northernmost of China's two major rivers, has run dry for a part of each year since 1985, with the dry period becoming progressively longer. In 1997, it failed to make it to the sea for 226 days. The Nile, the largest river in the Middle East, has little water left when it reaches the sea.[2]

Water tables are now falling on every continent. Among the food-producing regions where aquifers are being depleted are the U.S. southern Great Plains; the north China plain, which produces nearly 40 percent of China's grain; and most of India. Wherever water tables are falling today, there will be water supply cutbacks tomorrow, as aquifers are eventually depleted.[3]

Worldwide, some 70 percent of the water pumped from underground or diverted from rivers is used for irrigation, 20 percent is used for industrial purposes, and 10 percent is for residential use. Water use patterns vary widely by region. In Europe, for example, where agriculture is largely rainfed, water withdrawals are dominated by industrial use. In Asia, in contrast, irrigation accounts for 85 percent of all water use.[4]

As countries press against the limits of their water supplies, the competition among sectors intensifies. The economics of water use does not favor agriculture. One thousand tons of water can be used to produce one ton of wheat worth $200 or to expand industrial output by $14,000. This ratio of 70 to 1 explains why industry almost always wins in the competition with agriculture for water.[5]

As the growing demand for water collides with the limits of supply, countries typically satisfy rising urban and residential demands by diverting water from irrigation. They then import grain to offset the loss of irrigation water. Since it takes at least 1,000 tons of water to produce a ton of grain, importing grain becomes the most efficient way to import water. North Africa and the Middle East—a region where population growth is rapid and every country faces water shortages—has become the world's fastest-growing grain import market during the 1990s. In 1997, the water required to produce the grain and other food-stuffs imported into the region was roughly equal to the annual flow of the Nile River.[6]

In both China and India, the two countries that together dominate world irrigated agriculture, substantial cutbacks in irrigation water supplies lie ahead. The combination of aquifer depletion in key countries such as these and the growing diversion of irrigation water to nonfarm uses makes it unlikely that there will be much, if any, increase in irrigated area over the long term. Already the irrigated area per person has been slowly declining since 1978, falling from a historical high of 0.047 hectares per person to 0.045 hectares in 1996—a drop of 4 percent. If the total irrigated area remains at roughly 263 million hectares until 2050, this key figure will fall to 0.030 hectares per person in 2050—declining by an additional 33 percent. (See Figure 3–1.) Such a shrinkage will pose a formidable challenge to the world's farmers. This dramatic worldwide decline in irrigated area per person meshes with a recent projection by Sandra Postel in *BioScience*, which concluded that by 2025 the additional irrigation water needed in world agriculture will be equal to the annual flow of 24 Nile Rivers.[7]

David Seckler and his colleagues at the International Water Management Institute project that a billion people will be living in countries facing absolute water scarcity by 2025. These nations will lack water to main-

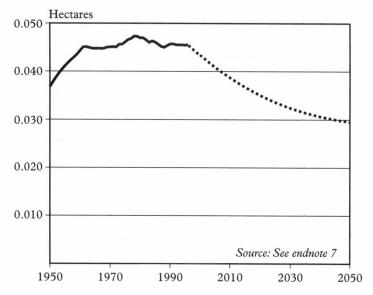

FIGURE 3–1. *Global Irrigated Area Per Person, 1950–96,*
With Projections to 2050

tain 1990 levels of food production per person from
irrigated area, even with high irrigation efficiency, and
to meet the needs for domestic, industrial, and environmental purposes as well. They will have to reduce
water use in agriculture in order to satisfy residential
and industrial water needs. The resulting decline in
food production will force them to import more food,
assuming it is available. Although detailed water projections by sector for each country are not available for
2050, the number of water-deprived people will be far
greater than in 2025 if the world continues on the U.N.
medium population trajectory. The bottom line is that
if we are facing a future of water scarcity, then we are
also facing a future of food scarcity.[8]

4

Biodiversity

As human population has surged this century, the populations of numerous other species have tumbled, many to the point of extinction. Indeed, we live amid the greatest extinction of plant and animal life since the dinosaurs disappeared some 65 million years ago, with species losses at 100 to 1,000 times the natural rate. But we are not just witnesses to a rare historic event, we are actually its cause. The leading sources of today's species loss—habitat alteration, invasions by exotic species, pollution, and overhunting—are all a function of human activities.[1]

A series of studies over the past decade by the World Conservation Union–IUCN has documented the stresses facing a broad range of species, with disturbing conclusions. Human activities have pushed the percentage of mammals, amphibians, and fish that are in "immediate danger" of extinction into double digits. (See Table 4–1.)[2]

Habitat loss, the principal cause of species extinction, is especially problematic in coastal areas, which are home to 60 percent of the world's population and are particularly rich in biodiversity. Coastal wetlands nurture two thirds of all commercially caught fish, for example. And coral reefs have the second highest concentration of biodiversity in the world, after tropical rainforests. But human encroachment and pollution are degrading these areas: roughly half of the world's salt marshes and mangrove swamps have been eliminated or radically altered, and two thirds of the world's coral reefs have been degraded, 10 percent of them "beyond recognition." As coastal migration continues—coastal dwellers will account for an increasingly disproportionate share of world population in the decades ahead—the pressures on these productive habitats will likely increase.[3]

TABLE 4–1. *Share of Species Worldwide Classified as Threatened*

	Share of Species That Is		
	In Immediate Danger of Extinction	Vulnerable to Extinction	Total Share of Species Threatened with Extinction
	(percent)		
Birds	4	7	11
Mammals	11	14	25
Reptiles	8	12	20
Amphibians	10	15	25
Fish	13	21	34

SOURCE: See endnote 2.

Habitat is also lost to agriculture, as population growth increases the demand for food. Ten percent of the world's land area is now dedicated to crops; most of that land has been stripped of the species diversity that characterized its wild state. This reduction in diversity is exacerbated by modern farming methods, which spread the same high-yielding crop varieties across vast areas in order to maximize production. In Bangladesh, for example, a single wheat variety was planted across two thirds of the country's wheat area in 1983.[4]

As population-induced dependence on high-yielding strains grows, the variety of cultivated crops falls. China grew 10,000 varieties of wheat in 1949, but only 1,000 in the 1970s, and Mexico, the birthplace of corn, cultivates only 20 percent as many corn varieties today as in 1930. Unless samples of the abandoned crop species are preserved in seedbanks, many become candidates for extinction: in the United States, two thirds of all rare and endangered plants are close relatives of cultivated varieties.[5]

The loss of wild crop varieties eliminates genetic material that is an important source of crop robustness. Genes from wild varieties are used to give cultivated varieties desired characteristics such as resistance to pests, drought, or disease. The combination of a dwindling pool of genetic resources and increasing dependence on monocultures makes growing populations increasingly vulnerable to crop failure—and to the very food shortages that high-yielding varieties were designed to avoid.[6]

Related to loss of habitat is the growing incidence of plant, animal, insect, and microbial invasions of ecosystems worldwide as human interchange increases. These "exotic species" sometimes dominate local ecosystems, eliminating native species and reducing overall diversity. Exotics are implicated in 68 percent of all fish extinctions in the United States in this century, for example. Growth in human travel and commerce explains many accidental invasions by exotics, but foreign species are also deliberately introduced into gardens, plantation forests, and aquaculture systems. Although only 1 percent of exotics cause widespread damage, exotic species are the second leading cause, after habitat destruction, of species loss worldwide.[7]

Other, often diffuse effects of expanded human activities also disrupt ecosystems. Nitrogen, for example, is now made available to plants at more than twice the preindustrial rate as a result of fertilizer production, cultivation of nitrogen-fixing crops, and the nitrous oxides that result from the burning of fossil fuels. This overfertilization of the Earth favors some species at the expense of others, leading to a reduction in diversity and resiliency of land and aquatic ecosystems.[8]

Likewise, greenhouse gas emissions could disrupt ecosystems on a vast scale. As with nitrogen, increased levels of atmospheric carbon may favor some species over others: annuals over perennials, for example, or deciduous trees over evergreens. To the extent that greenhouse gases induce changes in global climate, many species may be at risk as habitats shift or shrink, and as some life forms, such as insects or animals, adapt and migrate more quickly than others, such as plants. And as sea levels rise with a change in climate, ecosystems such as coastal wetlands could be destroyed.[9]

5

Energy

It has been scarcely 200 years—the dawn of the Industrial Revolution—since humans abandoned sole reliance on firewood, other biomass fuels, and direct sunlight to meet daily energy needs. In the past half-century, global demand for energy multiplied more than five times—over twice as fast as population—as industrial nations burned coal, oil, and natural gas to fuel their economies. (See Figure 5–1.) Over the next half-century, world energy demands are projected to continue expanding well beyond population growth, as developing countries try to catch up with industrial nations.[1]

The dizzying growth in energy use projected for the next 50 years in both industrial and developing nations stems almost exclusively from rising energy use per

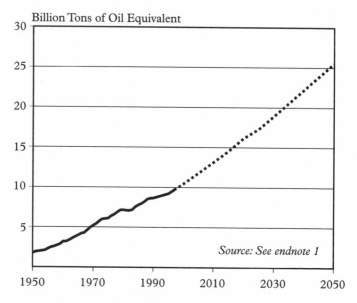

Billion Tons of Oil Equivalent

Source: See endnote 1

FIGURE 5-1. *Global Energy Use, 1950–97,*
With Projections to 2050

person. Based on projections from the U.S. Department of Energy (DOE) and the Intergovernmental Panel on Climate Change (IPCC), a full 86 percent of the global increase results from rising consumption per person—related to changes in affluence and standards of living—while population growth accounts for just 14 percent.[2]

Annual energy consumption in the developing world is projected to grow by 336 percent—nearly four times faster than population—over the next 50 years, from 3,499 million tons of oil equivalent to 15,255 million tons. And industrial-nation energy demand is expected to nearly double, to 10,247 million tons by 2050, despite a population decrease over the same period.[3]

Though rising per capita consumption accounts for most of the growth in energy demand in poorer nations, different population trajectories can still have dramatic effects on future demands. For example, assuming the same growth in per capita energy demand, moving to the low U.N. population projection will reduce total energy demands from developing countries by 2,792 million tons of oil equivalent—the output of nearly 3,000 average-sized coal-fired power plants.[4]

In the next 50 years, the greatest growth in energy demand will come where economic activity is projected to be highest: in Asia, where consumption is expected to grow 361 percent, though population will grow by just 50 percent. Energy consumption in Latin America and Africa is projected to increase by 340 percent and 326 percent, respectively. Lower rates of population growth in Asia, compared with Latin America and Africa, mean that energy use per person will increase most in Asia. Nonetheless, in all three regions, local pressures on energy sources, ranging from forests to fossil fuel reserves to waterways, will be significant.[5]

When per capita energy consumption is high, even a low rate of population growth can have a large absolute effect on total energy demand. In the United States, for example, where current per capita energy demand is nearly double that in other industrial nations and over 13 times that in developing countries, the 71 million people projected to be added in the next 50 years will boost energy demands by 758 million tons of oil equivalent—roughly the same as the present energy consumption of Africa and Latin America.

World energy use per person doubled between 1950 and 1973, before confronting a short-term slowdown when restricted exports from oil-producing nations drove up energy prices. Another price shock, combined with a global economic recession, resulted in the slow-down of the early 1980s. The most recent stumbling block in energy growth followed the 1989 revolution in Eastern Europe, when energy use in the former Soviet states plummeted. Although DOE and IPCC project substantial future global growth, similar forces may act to check such a development.[7]

World oil production per person reached a high in 1979 and has since declined 23 percent. Moreover, estimates of when global oil production will peak range from 2010 to 2025, signaling future price shocks as long as oil remains the world's dominant fuel. Although people born in 1950 saw per capita oil production quickly double in a few short decades, those born in 2000 are likely to see it cut in half, dropping below 1950 levels.[8]

For the estimated 2 billion who are still off the grid—and also experiencing high rates of population growth—the principal barrier to meeting future energy demands may be infrastructure. Communities without a reliable supply of water or an adequate system for waste disposal may also fall short in connection to power supplies.[9]

Yet it will not necessarily be the scarcity of fuel that constrains future growth in energy consumption, but rather concerns about climate change, air quality, and water quality—concerns that our past and current energy habits have largely neglected. A shift to renewable energy sources, such as solar energy and wind power, holds great promise for meeting future energy demands without adverse ecological consequences.

6

Oceanic Fish Catch

From 1950 until 1988, the oceanic fish catch soared from 19 million to 88 million tons, expanding much faster than population. The per capita catch increased from less than 8 kilograms in 1950 to the historical peak of 17 kilograms in 1988, more than doubling. (See Figure 6–1.) Since 1988, however, growth in the catch has slowed, falling behind that of population. Between 1988 and 1997, the catch per person declined to just over 16 kilograms, a drop of some 4 percent.[1]

This fivefold growth in the human appetite for seafood since 1950 has pushed the catch of most oceanic fisheries to their sustainable limits or beyond. Marine biologists believe that the oceans cannot sustain an annual catch of much more than the current take of 97 million tons.[2]

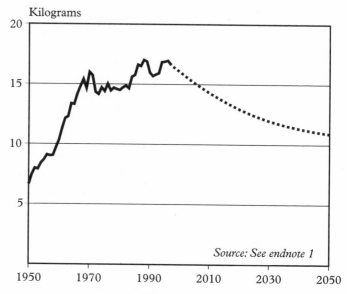

FIGURE 6–1. *World Fish Catch Per Person, 1950–97, With Projections to 2050*

As we near the end of the twentieth century, overfishing has become the rule, not the exception. Of the 15 major oceanic fisheries, 11 are in decline. The catch of Atlantic cod—long a dietary mainstay for West Europeans—has fallen by some 70 percent since peaking in 1968. Since 1970, bluefin tuna stocks in the West Atlantic have dropped 80 percent.[3]

The next half-century is likely to be marked by the disappearance of some species from markets, a decline in the quality of seafood caught, higher prices, and more conflicts among countries over access to fisheries. Over the last two decades, a growing share of the catch has consisted of inferior species, some of which were not even considered edible in times past.[4]

The growing scarcity of the species at the top of the food chain is reflected in rising prices. Poor people who once ate fish because they could not afford meat now find that meat is often less expensive than seafood. Although most price rises are moderate, some are extreme—going far beyond anything we could have earlier imagined. The decline of the bluefin tuna population in the Atlantic, for instance, has occasionally pushed prices for a 300-kilogram tuna above $80,000 as top-of-the-line sushi restaurants in Japan compete for the few of these giant fish that are available.[5]

This growing competition for limited resources has led to ongoing conflicts among countries. The United Nations recorded more than 100 such disputes in 1997. These are evident in the cod wars between Norwegian and Icelandic ships, between Canada and Spain over turbot off Canada's eastern coast, between China and the Marshall Islands in Micronesia, between Argentina and Taiwan over Falkland Island fisheries, and between Indonesia and the Philippines in the Celebes. A Greenpeace spokesperson notes there are "tuna wars in the northeast Atlantic, crab wars in the North Pacific, squid wars in the southwest Atlantic, salmon wars in the North Pacific, and pollock wars in the Sea of Okhotsk." Although these disputes make it into the world news only rarely, they are now an almost daily occurrence. Indeed, historians may record more fishery conflicts during one year in the 1990s than during the entire nineteenth century.[6]

One of the consequences of modern fishing technologies, whether it is the use of drift nets or bottom-scouring fishing techniques, is an increase in the bycatch—the inadvertent catch of unwanted species. This oceanic equivalent of clearcutting is damaging fisheries on an unprecedented scale.[7]

With the oceans now pushed to their limits, future growth in the demand for seafood can be satisfied only by fish farming. As a result, aquacultural output has increased from 7 million tons in 1984 to an estimated 28 million tons in 1997. Most of this growth in catch is based on just a few species, such as carp, which constitute most of the aquacultural harvest in China, and catfish, which dominate fish farming in the United States. As the world turns to fish farming to satisfy its needs, fish begin to compete with livestock and poultry for feedstuffs such as grain, soybean meal, and fishmeal.[8]

Given that the oceanic fish catch is apparently now close to or beyond its sustainable limit, it is a relatively simple matter to determine the future oceanic catch per person. With each year, this will decline by roughly the amount of population growth, dropping to 10.9 kilograms per person in 2050, a decline to less than two thirds the 1988 peak of 17.0 kilograms. Those of us born before 1950 have enjoyed a doubling of the seafood catch per person, while those born in recent years are likely to witness a decline of nearly one half during their lifetimes.[9]

7

Jobs

Since mid-century, the world's labor force has more than doubled—from 1.2 billion people to 2.7 billion, outstripping the growth in job creation. As a result, the United Nations International Labour Organisation estimates that nearly 1 billion people, approximately one third of the global work force, are unemployed or underemployed (working but not earning enough to meet basic needs). Over the next half-century, the world will need to create more than 1.7 billion jobs—all of them in the developing world—just to maintain current levels of employment.[1]

As economists often note, while population growth may boost labor demand (through economic activity and demand for goods), it will most definitely boost labor supply. During the next 50 years, almost 35 million people will enter the global labor force—defined as those between the ages of 15 and 65 seeking work—each year. Some 1.7 billion additional jobs will need to be created to absorb these new would-be workers. (See Table 7–1.) The most pressing needs will be found in the world's poorest nations—a sobering example of the vicious cycle linking poverty and population growth.[2]

As the children of today represent the workers of tomorrow, the interaction between population growth and jobs is most acute in nations with young populations. Nations such as Peru, Mexico, Indonesia, and Zambia with more than half their population below the age of 25 will feel the burden of this labor flood. In the Middle East and Africa, 40 percent of the population is under the age of 15. Since new entrants into the labor force were born at least 15 years ago, measures to

TABLE 7–1. *World Labor Force, 1995, With Projections to 2050*

	1995	2050	Additional Jobs Required, 1995 to 2050	Change, 1995–2050
	(million)			(percent)
World	2,735	4,455	1,720	76
Industrial Countries	598	513	−84	−14
Developing Countries	2,127	3,928	1,806	85
Least Developed Countries[1]	258	866	607	235

[1] 48 poorest nations in the world, based on per capita GNP.
SOURCE: U.N. projections of population and dependency ratios, and ILO projections of regional work activity rates.

reduce population growth have a delayed effect on the growth of the labor force.[3]

Nowhere is the employment challenge greater than in Africa, where at least 40 percent of the population lives in absolute poverty. Although 8 million people entered the sub-Saharan work force in 1998, in just two decades this resource-scarce region will have to absorb more than 16 million—twice as many—new entrants each year. At current growth rates, the size of the labor force in sub-Saharan Africa will more than triple by 2050. Nigeria's labor force is projected to grow by 189 percent and Ethiopia's will soar by 268 percent—both faster than growth of the general population.[4]

As a result of unprecedented population growth and increasing acceptance of female participation in the work force, the number of people working in the Middle East and North Africa, a region already plagued by double-digit unemployment rates, will double in the next 50 years. In Algeria, where unemployment stands at 22 percent, the labor force is growing at a staggering 4.2 percent annually, and the number seeking work will more than double by 2050.[5]

Nations throughout Asia will also see phenomenal increases in the numbers seeking work, including Pakistan, where the work force will grow from 70 million in 1998 to 199 million by 2050. Over the next 25 years, India will add nearly 10 million to its work force each year. During the same period, China will add nearly 6 million annually due to population growth alone, compounding the work shortages caused by the current flood of migrants to China's coastal cities and by massive layoffs—estimated at more than 30 million—as state-run operations are scaled back.[6]

Nations are hard-pressed to educate and train rapidly growing numbers of young people in marketable skills for the global workplace. Throughout the world, young people entering the work force are increasingly faced with unemployment and social marginalization. In most societies, unemployment rates for those under 25 are substantially higher than for older people. And persistent high levels of unemployment in many European nations with stable populations indicate the policy challenges of providing jobs even without rapid population growth.[7]

Surplus farmland once served as a traditional source of employment for growing populations, as new land could be plowed to generate work and income. However, global per capita grainland has dropped by half—and considerably more in certain nations—since 1950. Moreover, the global exodus of job seekers from the countryside fuels an already severe unemployment problem. Heavily reliant on natural capital in the past, future job creation will require massive amounts of capital to accelerate job creation in the industrial and service sectors.[8]

As the balance between the demand and supply of labor is tipped by population growth, wages—the price of labor—tend to decrease. And in a situation of labor surplus, the quality of jobs may not improve as fast, for workers will settle for longer hours, fewer benefits, and less control over work activities. In an increasingly globalized labor market, surplus labor anywhere will weaken labor's bargaining power everywhere.[9]

Employment is the key to obtaining food, housing, health services, and education, in addition to providing self-respect and self-fulfillment. Rising numbers of unemployed people could drive global poverty and hunger to precarious levels, fueling political instability.

8

Infectious Disease

Historically, the spread, prevalence, and very existence of contagious disease have wholly depended on the growth and concentration of human populations. The unprecedented population densities in fourteenth-century Europe, for example, led to the plague outbreak that claimed the lives of one fourth of the population. And though the last half-century has witnessed substantial worldwide success in combating many past scourges—such as polio and smallpox—infectious diseases still claim more lives than any other group of diseases. (See Table 8–1.) The prevailing demographic trends continue to create a crowded human "medium" that both invites and is vulnerable to infection.[1]

The share of humanity living in cities with more than 1 million people has surged from less than 5 percent in

TABLE 8–1. *Profile of the World's Major Infectious Diseases, 1997*

Disease	Deaths (million)	Global Trend
Acute respiratory infections	3.7	Mainly pneumonia, these diseases are major killers of children under age five; nearly 400 million new cases each year; deteriorating air quality in urban areas, inadequate housing conditions, and malnutrition increase risks.
Tuberculosis	2.9	An estimated one third of humanity (2 billion people) carry the TB bacteria; resistance to antibiotics and AIDS have led to its resurgence; growing rapidly in Asia and sub-Saharan Africa.
Diarrheal diseases	2.5	Some 4 billion new cases each year, largely due to inadequate sanitation and contaminated water; major killers of children worldwide: 25 percent of deaths of children under age five in Asia.
AIDS	2.3	Nearly 40 million infected worldwide; 25 percent of adult population infected in some African nations; epidemic growing rapidly in Asia and Latin America; no cure.
Malaria	2.1	Has resurged worldwide as resistance to antimalarial drugs and mosquito-killing insecticides grows; prevalence dictated by mosquito populations, which are favored by dense urban settlements.

SOURCE: See endnote 1.

1900 to nearly 40 percent today, creating the ideal setting for the resurgence of old infectious diseases as well as the development of new ones. Pathogens can more readily establish in large populations, since all infectious diseases require a critical number of vulnerable individuals in order to take root and spread.[2]

Overcrowding—the increased proximity of suscepti-
ble individuals—is a principal risk factor for the incidence and spread of all major infectious diseases,
including tuberculosis, dengue fever, malaria, and
acute respiratory illnesses, which are unable to spread
and survive in low population densities. Key disease
carriers, such as insects and rats, thrive in crowded
urban settings, further facilitating spread.[3]

Aside from sheer growth and increasing density, the
urbanization under way in developing nations is often
accompanied by deteriorating health indicators and
increased exposure to disease risk factors.[4]

Access to clean water, good hygiene, and adequate
housing are sorely lacking in developing nations. As a
result, waterborne infections such as cholera and other
diarrheal diseases account for 90 percent of all infectious diseases in developing countries—and 40 percent
of all deaths in some nations—but only a fraction of the
industrial-nation burden. Although these infections are
easily preventable if adequate water and sanitation are
available, the vast majority of the world's population
are lifelong victims.[5]

In both industrial and developing nations, inci-
dences of a wide range of infectious diseases, including
tuberculosis, diarrheal diseases, and HIV/AIDS, are
considerably higher in urban slums—where poverty
and compromised health define the way of life—than
in the rest of the city. These areas can serve as a
perpetual reservoir of disease or disease vectors, placing other parts of the city at risk of an outbreak and
allowing the disease to continue evolving, often into a
deadlier strain.[6]

A wide range of human activities whose scale is often

linked to population growth—including forest clearing, animal husbandry, and dam building—favor the presence of organisms that carry disease. The prevalence of schistosomiasis in Egypt, for instance, exploded from 5 percent in 1968 to more than 70 percent today after the Aswan Dam project in 1967 created vast bodies of standing fresh water, the preferred habitat for the snail that carries the disease.[7]

We know how to eradicate most infectious diseases, though implementation is often lacking. Competing demands for limited administrative and fiscal resources make it harder to provide basic preventive care, including immunization and regular health checkups. When the 1990 collapse of the Soviet health care system disabled vaccination programs, diphtheria ran rampant throughout Russia for the first time this century. And in Zimbabwe, where there is no national AIDS program, military expenditures expand even as one in four adults is HIV-positive.[8]

In many poor nations, where existing public health infrastructure is already overtaxed, population growth feeds the epidemiological fire. More than half the citizens in many large, fast-growing nations, including Bangladesh, the Congo, Ethiopia, and Pakistan, have no access to basic health care.[9]

In the decades ahead, public health officials everywhere face an array of challenges, including an expanded range of tropical diseases due to climate change and the misuse of antibiotics that encourages resistance. Migration and long-distance transport link the world's microbes, so that no nation is immune to epidemics elsewhere. Increases in population numbers and densities will make the threat of infectious disease ever more acute.

9

Cropland

Since mid-century, global population has grown much faster than the cropland area. The trend is likely to continue in the next century, dropping cropland per person to historically low levels. The ever smaller per capita cropland base will make food self-sufficiency impossible for many countries, and will test the capacity of international markets to meet a growing demand for imported food.[1]

For millennia, farmers satisfied rising food demand by bringing new land under the plow. But by mid-century cropland expansion could no longer meet the food needs of an increasingly populous and prosperous world. The 10,000-year era of steady expansion was over, and a new era began that stressed raising land productivity. As this high-yielding era shows signs of

faltering, concern over the shrinking supply of cropland per person looms ever larger.[2]

Since mid-century, grain area—which serves as a
proxy for cropland in general—has increased by some
19 percent, but global population has grown 132 percent, seven times faster. Largely as a result, grain area
per person has fallen by half since 1950, from 0.24 to
0.12 hectares—about one sixth the size of a soccer
field. (See Figure 9–1.) Assuming that grain area
remains constant, grain area per person will fall to 0.08
hectares by 2050. In crowded industrial countries such
as Japan, Taiwan, and South Korea, grain area per capita today is smaller than the area of a tennis court.[3]

As grain area per person falls, more and more
nations risk losing the capacity to feed themselves. The
trend is illustrated starkly in the world's three fastest-
growing large countries. Having already seen per capita grain area shrink by 38–56 percent between 1950
and 1998, Pakistan, Nigeria, and Ethiopia can expect a
further 55–63 percent loss by 2050—a conservative
projection that assumes no further losses of agricultural land. The result will be three countries with a combined population of more than 750 million whose grain
area per person will be only 300–700 square meters, a
third or less than the area in 1950.[4]

The historical record suggests that such a small area
per person will send a substantial share of a country's
people to world markets for their food. Consider the
experience of six countries in East Asia whose per capita grain area currently ranges from 200 to 600 square
meters per person. Sri Lanka relies on imports for
more than a third of its grain, while Japan, Taiwan,
South Korea, and Malaysia buy more than 70 percent
of their grain from abroad. North Korea is the only one

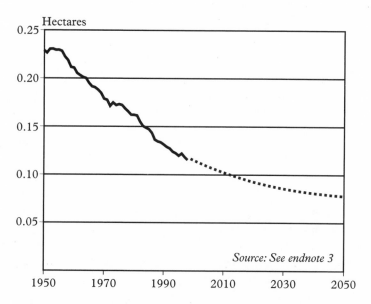

FIGURE 9–1. *World Grain Harvested Area Per Person, 1950–98, With Projections to 2050*

of the six that does not import heavily (it gets less than 20 percent of its grain requirements from abroad), but its population is poorly fed—indeed, on the verge of starvation.[5]

The concern is that population growth will push many nations—not just the three fastest-growing ones—below the threshold of 600–700 square meters in coming decades. In Asia alone, where grain area per person stands at 800 square meters, 11 countries are poised to cross this threshold by 2050, and many of them much sooner. As this process unfolds, the number of people who will turn to foreign markets for their food will likely jump sharply. These countries will find an increasingly tight international grain market, with nations from the Middle East, North Africa, and other regions already buying a third or more of their grain overseas.[6]

In addition to per capita losses, population growth can lead to degradation of cropland, reducing its productivity or even eliminating it from production. As a country's population density increases and good farmland becomes scarce, poor farmers are forced onto ecologically vulnerable land such as hillsides and tropical forest. In the Philippines, for example, hillside agriculture accounted for only 10 percent of all agricultural land in 1960, but 30 percent in 1987. Because it is highly erodible, hillside land is easily damaged; worldwide, some 160 million hectares of hillside farmland—11 percent of cropland—were characterized in 1989 as "severely eroded." Similarly, population pressure can force peasants to overfarm the poor soils of tropical forests. After being cleared and farmed for a few years, these soils typically require fallow periods of 20–25 years, but population pressures keep poor farmers on the same land for far longer than the soil can support, cutting fallow periods to just a few years in some areas of tropical Africa and Asia.[7]

Finally, population pressures on a fixed base of land can result in rural landlessness. In Bangladesh, for example, landlessness among rural households rose from 35 percent in 1960 to 53 percent in the early 1990s. Interestingly, Bangladesh is regarded as a success in slowing population expansion, as its growth rate declined from 2.8 percent in the late 1970s to 1.5 percent in the early 1990s. But its success came too late to prevent an increase in rural landlessness, highlighting the need to work sooner, rather than later, for population stabilization.[8]

10

Forests

Global losses of forest area have marched in step with population growth for much of human history. The two trends rose slowly for millennia, turned upward in recent centuries, and accelerated sharply after 1900. Indeed, 75 percent of the historical growth in global population and an estimated 75 percent of the loss in global forested area have occurred in the twentieth century. The correlation makes sense, given the additional need for farmland, pastureland, and forest products as human numbers expand. But since 1950, the advent of mass consumption of forest products has quickened the pace of deforestation. (See Table 10–1.)[1]

Several datasets suggest that population pressure is still closely linked with deforestation. In Latin America, for example, ranching is the single largest cause of

TABLE 10–1. *Forested Area Per Capita, 1995,*
With Projections to 2050

Region	Forested Area Per Capita	
	1995	2050
	(hectares)	
Africa	0.32	0.13
Asia	0.12	0.08
Europe and Russia	1.10	1.28
North and Central America	2.07	1.54
Oceania	3.32	2.01
South America	2.14	1.27
World	0.59	0.37

SOURCE: See endnote 1.

deforestation. Because most meat produced in Latin America is consumed there, and because meat consumption per person has been largely unchanged for several decades, it is possible that expanding population is the principal reason for ranching-related deforestation. In addition, analysts at the World Resources Institute estimate that overgrazing and overcollection of firewood—which are often a function of a growing population—are degrading some 14 percent of the world's threatened frontier forests (large areas of virgin forest). And a U.N. Food and Agriculture Organization study showed a one-to-one correlation between population growth and fuelwood consumption in 16 Asian countries between 1961 and 1994.[2]

On the other hand, deforestation created by the demand for forest products tracks more closely with rising per capita consumption in recent decades. Global use of paper and paperboard per person, for example, has doubled (or nearly tripled) since 1961, and most of the increase has come in wealthy countries with low or even stable levels of population growth. Europe,

Japan, and North America, with 19 percent of global population, consume 63 percent of the world's paper and paperboard and nearly half its industrial wood.[3]

Although consumption and population growth have operated somewhat independently in the late twentieth century, the two forces could coincide in the developing world in coming decades, with substantial consequences for forests. Developing-country paper consumption is less than one tenth the level found in industrial nations, suggesting that large increases in consumption are likely as these nations prosper. (It also suggests that greater economy is needed in industrial countries.) With 80 percent of the world's people, and as home to all of the increase in population in coming decades, even modest growth in per capita paper and wood consumption in developing countries could place substantial pressure on forests. If paper were used by the entire world in 2050 at today's industrial-nation rates, paper production would need to jump more than eightfold over 1996 levels.[4]

This projected growth is unsustainable, given that global use of forest products is already near or beyond the limits of sustainable use. Using data on sustainable forest yields, and assuming that virgin forests are left intact, researchers at Friends of the Earth UK have determined that production of forest products for the world is 25 percent beyond the most restrictive estimates for sustainable consumption. (Many forests, of course, are already logged well beyond sustainable levels.) The most optimistic assessment would allow for a further 35-percent growth in consumption. Even that spells trouble, however, given a projected global population increase of some 47 percent over the next half-century, and given the likely increase in consumption from rising prosperity. Lower consumption of forest products and increased recycling in industrial countries can make room for a more prosperous developing world to enjoy the products of the world's forests, but the task will be made easier if population growth everywhere is stabilized sooner rather than later.[5]

If population and consumption eat into the world's forests, the resulting loss of forest services reduces, in turn, a country's capacity to support its population. Forests provide habitat to a diverse selection of wildlife; tropical forests, for example, are home to more than 50 percent of the world's plant and animal species. And as storehouses of carbon, forests are key to regulating climate. Deforestation leads to huge releases of carbon: an estimated one quarter of the world's carbon emissions come from forest clearing. Loss of these macroservices undermines the stability and resiliency of the global environment on which economies—and populations—depend. In addition, forests provide services vital to a local population, such as control of erosion, steady provision of water across rainy and dry seasons, and regulation of rainfall. Taken together, the loss of these services due to deforestation can upset local economies and subject local populations to economic instability.[6]

11

Housing

Over the past half-century, the world's housing stock has grown roughly in step with population. Yet for more and more people worldwide, adequate and affordable housing remains beyond reach, driving some into substandard dwellings and slums and others onto the street. Without renewed government commitments to provide housing, this situation stands to worsen, for housing needs worldwide are projected to nearly double over the next 50 years.[1]

Although industrial nations currently occupy a disproportionately large share of the world's households relative to their population, virtually all future growth will occur in developing countries, where housing requirements will more than double by the middle of the twenty-first century. (See Table 11–1.) This phe-

TABLE 11–1. *Number of Households Worldwide, 1995, With Projections to 2050*

	1995	2050	Additional Housing Required	Change, 1995–2050
	(million)			(percent)
World	1,403	2,466	1,063	76
Industrial Countries	439	510	70	16
Developing Countries	964	1,957	993	103

SOURCE: See endnote 2.

nomenal growth results from the potent synergy between population growth and a shift toward fewer people per household—a trend that is especially pronounced where economic growth is rapid.[2]

Projected housing requirements by HABITAT, the United Nations Centre for Human Settlements, assume roughly a 30-percent reduction in people per household over the next 50 years. These figures do not consider possible checks in housing growth, such as materials or financial constraints, intensified land competition, or increased poverty. Our own projections assume that household size will indeed decrease, as fertility rates drop and as nuclear families continue to replace extended ones, but by a more modest 15 percent.

Over the next 50 years, housing needs in Africa and the Middle East are expected to increase more than threefold, with tremendous gains in the region's most populous nations; demands are to increase 2.5 times in Nigeria and 3.5 times in Ethiopia. Although less dramatic percentage increases are expected in Asia, the doubling of households in the region will require nearly 700 million additional homes by 2050. Still, some countries there, such as Pakistan and neighboring Afghanistan, will see housing needs increase nearly three and a half times.[3]

The projected growth in housing needs becomes all the more daunting given that rapid population growth—combined with rapid urban growth—has already left a large share of the world's population without adequate housing. Habitat estimates that at least 600 million urban dwellers and more than 1 billion rural dwellers in Africa, Asia, and Latin America live in housing that is "so overcrowded and of such poor quality with such inadequate provision for water, sanitation, drainage, and garbage collection that their health and lives are continually at risk."[4]

As the supply of housing falls behind demand, the quality of available housing tends to deteriorate. Cheaper, less durable materials, such as scrap metal and cardboard, are substituted for more expensive, weather-resistant materials, such as concrete and wood. Fierce competition in swelling urban areas for desirable land can eliminate all hope of low-income households acquiring a plot for housing. As choice of location dwindles, shantytowns and other low-quality settlements develop on marginal land ill suited for housing. From New York to Beijing, cities face land and materials constraints even as their populations swell.[5]

At the same time, housing area per person continues to increase in certain nations and among the more affluent segments of other nations, placing additional stress on prime space and building materials. In the United States, Western Europe, and Japan, floor space per person has more than doubled in new single-family homes since mid-century. The global disparity in floor space per person—Washington, D.C., at the high end with 70

square meters per person, and most of humanity at
around 9 square meters per person—will likely mimic
the growing global disparity in income, as wealthy
households scale up and poorer households fill up.[6]

Housing can provide a connection to a supply of fresh
water and sanitation facilities. But as its quality deteriorates, so do these basic amenities. Half the world's people are without access to sanitation and nearly this
many—2.7 billion—are without a reliable source of safe
drinking water. Shortages of housing that provides these
basic services are most acute in cities, where rapid
urbanization and high population densities place
heightened demands on infrastructure. And still housing needs will soar in the regions of the world where
access to water and sanitation are most constrained.[7]

The ultimate manifestation of population growth
outstripping the supply of housing is homelessness. The
United Nations estimates that at least 100 million of
the world's people—roughly the same as the population
of Mexico—have no home; the number tops 1 billion
if those with especially insecure or temporary accom-
modations, such as squatters, are included. In many
developing countries, squatter communities are home
to 30–60 percent of the urban population. There are
some 250,000 pavement dwellers in Bombay alone. In
Latin America, *los niños de las calles* (children of the
streets) humans who are born, live, and die in the
streets—are common in all major cities. Homelessness
in industrial nations undergoing little population
growth highlights the added role of housing policy in
ensuring universal shelter.[8]

Unless nations deal with pervasive housing policy
shortfalls and move to lower population trajectories,
the ranks of homeless are likely to swell dramatically.

12

Climate Change

Over the last half-century, carbon emissions from fossil fuel burning expanded fourfold, boosting atmospheric concentrations of carbon dioxide, the principal greenhouse gas, by 30 percent over preindustrial levels. (See Figure 12–1.) All major scientific bodies acknowledge the likelihood that climate change due to the buildup of greenhouse gases in the atmosphere is indeed under way. The 15 warmest years on record have all occurred since 1979. And a preliminary estimate indicates that 1998 will be the warmest year on record. (See Figure 12–2.)[1]

The destabilization of our climate threatens more intense heat waves, more severe droughts and floods, more destructive storms, and more extensive forest fires. The related shifts in rainfall and temperature may

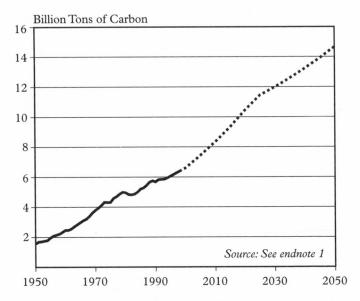

FIGURE 12–1. *Global Carbon Emissions, 1950–97,*
With Projections to 2050

jeopardize food production, the Earth's biological
diversity, and entire ecosystems, as well as human
health by expanding the ranges of tropical diseases.
Unless efforts to curb them are stepped up, carbon
emissions will continue to grow faster than population
over the next 50 years, driving the Earth's climate system into uncharted territory. The Intergovernmental
Panel on Climate Change (IPCC) estimates that an
eventual two-thirds reduction in global emissions is
needed to avoid a precarious doubling of atmospheric
carbon dioxide concentrations.[2]

Based on IPCC and U.S. Department of Energy
projections, annual emissions from developing countries will surge some 280 percent by 2050, while those

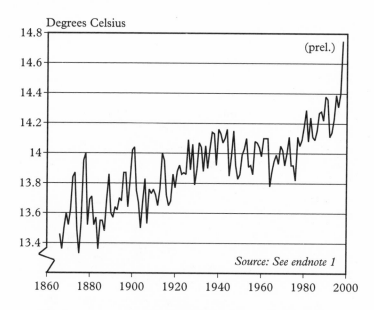

FIGURE 12–2. *Average Temperature at the Earth's Surface, 1866–1998*

from industrial nations—despite a decrease in population—will increase by 30 percent. Although annual emissions from industrial countries are currently twice as high as from developing ones, the latter are on target to eclipse the industrial world by 2020.[3]

Just as the lion's share of the global carbon emissions since 1950 resulted from a surge in emissions per person in present-day industrial nations, future global increases will be dominated by soaring per capita emissions in developing nations. These are due to more than double, from 0.5 tons of carbon per year in 2000—just one sixth of the industrial level—to 1.2 tons in 2050. Increased emissions per person—related to gains in prosperity—account for a full 77 percent of the projected rise in the developing world; the remaining 23 percent stems from population growth.[4]

Fossil fuel use accounts for roughly three quarters of world carbon emissions. As a result, regional growth in emissions tends to accompany increasing economic activity and related energy use. Emissions in China are projected to swell in the next half-century, as emissions per person soar from 0.77 tons of carbon to 2.81 tons due to a booming economy that is heavily reliant on coal. In Africa, in contrast, where emissions per person are expected to rise from 0.30 tons to 0.33 tons in 2050, nearly all of the threefold increase in emissions will come from population growth.[5]

The effects of population growth are most profound in countries where people are heavy emitters. For example, the 115 million people added to the population of the United States between 1950 and 1998—an increase of nearly 75 percent in just 45 years—account for more than one tenth of current global emissions. And the carbon emissions of the 71 million people who will be added to the U.S. population in the next 50 years roughly equal the emissions of the 1 billion people who will be added to Africa during that period.[6]

Deforestation and other land use changes account for the remainder of world carbon emissions. While the world's forests have stored vast amounts of carbon throughout much of human history, forest burning and clearing in the tropics release increasing amounts of carbon. Six months of fires in Asia in 1997 and 1998 released more carbon than Western Europe emits from fossil fuel burning in an entire year. The carbon contribution from this source will likely increase as the burgeoning human population continues to cut down forests.[7]

13

Materials

Because people need metal, wood, stone, chemicals, and other materials for their survival and enjoyment, population growth typically spurs increased materials use, which often leads to greater environmental degradation. But the materials impact of population growth depends largely on the lifestyles of the expanding population, and on how efficiently materials are used. Materials tend to be consumed heavily and wastefully in wealthy nations, making growth in human numbers in these countries more environmentally burdensome than the rapid growth in many poor countries.

In this century, prosperity and one-time use of most materials have been strong drivers of materials consumption. In the United States—one of the few countries with materials data back to 1900—population increased by 245 percent since the turn of the century, but materials use shot up by an astounding 1,673 percent. Global data on materials use is assembled only back to 1963, after industrialization and heavy materials use were well under way in many countries. Nevertheless, prosperity remained an important contributor. Global materials use surged by 141 percent between 1963 and 1995, compared with a 77-percent increase in world population in the same period.[1]

As developing countries prosper, they are also likely to use more materials just to provide basic services for their people. Nearly three fifths of the people in the developing world lack access to sanitation, a third do not have clean water, and a quarter live in inadequate housing.[2]

The infrastructure needed to provide these services can be materials-intensive: in the United States, for example, construction materials accounted for more than 72 percent of total materials use in 1995. Sprawling development makes materials use particularly high there, because more sewers, roads, police stations, and telephone lines are needed to service a given population, but even in densely constructed Asia, construction materials will be heavily used over the next decade. Spending on infrastructure to accommodate Asia's 3 billion people is projected to top $10 trillion over the next decade.[3]

Increased materials use, whether in wealthy or poor countries, will have a worsening environmental impact. Logging for wood and paper is implicated in deforestation, mining of metals has polluted rivers with toxic wastes, and chemicals poison people and animals, increase the risk of cancer, or are implicated in reproductive disorders. Even cement, a seemingly innocuous material, is tied to climate change: its production accounts for some 5 percent of global carbon emissions. And waste disposal generates its own problems. Landfills leach toxic liquids into groundwater supplies, and generate methane, a greenhouse gas with 20 times the global warming potential of carbon dioxide. Meanwhile, incinerators release dioxins, and dumped wastes pollute rivers, bays, and oceans.[4]

Many of these problems could worsen faster than the rate of increase in materials use. Over the life of a mine, for example, ore quality steadily decreases and more waste is generated per ton of metal extracted, increasing the threat to the environment. Alternatively, the environmental damage may occur suddenly: logging may eliminate species at a predictable rate for some time, but as an area approaches complete clearing, extinctions suddenly skyrocket. In sum, the environmental damage per ton of material used can sometimes be greater later in the extraction process than it was in the early stages.[5]

If everyone in the world lived at the U.S. level of materials consumption—nearly 11 tons per person annually—the projected population in 2050 would use some 95 billion tons of materials each year, nearly 10 times as much as today Even if the world consumes in 2050 at current per capita rates—allowing for no changes due to prosperity or increased efficiency—materials use would still rise by 50 percent. (See Figure 13–1.) Such increases would likely have severe consequences for the natural environment.[6]

Whether the demand for materials is generated in the industrial or the developing world, the environmental impact of materials extraction and use is increasingly felt in poorer countries. As mining regula-

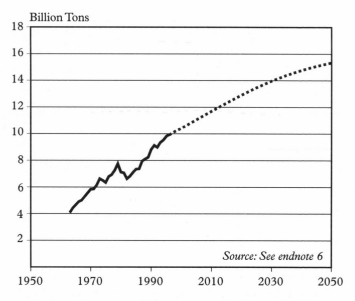

FIGURE 13–1. *World Materials Use, 1963–95,*
With Projections to 2050

tions have tightened in the United States, for example, companies have started to move to Latin America, where environmental laws are much less stringent. Likewise, the forests of the United States and Europe are now often protected, while those of Russia, Indonesia, Malaysia, and Central and South America are increasingly exploited. And air and water pollution standards in developing countries are less rigorous or less likely to be enforced than in industrial countries. Thus developing nations could find themselves not only with burgeoning populations, but also with increasingly spoiled environments.[7]

14

Urbanization

The world's cities are growing far faster than its population. Indeed, aside from the growth of population itself, urbanization is the dominant demographic trend of the half-century now ending. In 1950, 760 million of the world's people lived in cities. By 1998, this had at least tripled, to more than 2.7 billion. The number projected to live in cities by 2050, some 6.2 billion people, exceeds world population today. (See Table 14–1.)[1]

Urbanization on anything like the scale that we know today is historically quite recent. In 1800, only one city—London—had a million people. Today, 326 cities have at least that many people. And there are 16 megacities, those with 10 million or more residents. Tokyo is the largest, at 28 million. Mexico City is second, at 18 million. Bombay, São Paulo, and New York

TABLE 14–1. *World Population and Urbanization,*
1950–90, With Projections to 2050

Year	World Population	World Urban Population	Share of World Population That Is Urban
1950	2.6	0.8	30
1960	3.0	1.0	34
1970	3.7	1.4	37
1980	4.5	1.8	39
1990	5.3	2.3	43
2000	6.1	2.9	47
2010	6.8	3.5	52
2020	7.5	4.3	57
2030	8.1	5.0	61
2040	8.6	5.6	65
2050	8.9	6.2	69

SOURCE: See endnote 1.

City are close behind, with 17 million each. Rounding
out the list in descending size are Shanghai (14 million), Calcutta (13), Los Angeles (12), Buenos Aires
(12), Seoul (12), Beijing (12), Lagos (12), Osaka (11),
Delhi (11), Rio de Janeiro (10), and Dhaka (10).[2]

The rate of growth of cities in industrial countries
during the first century or so of the Industrial Revolution was relatively slow. Today's cities are growing
much faster. It took London 130 years to get from 1
million to 8 million. Mexico City made this jump in
just 30 years.[3]

Measured in annual growth, some cities, such as
Lagos, Nigeria, are growing at 5 percent a year; Bombay is growing at nearly 4 percent. The world's urban
population as a whole is growing by just over 1 million
people each week. This urban growth is fed by the natural increase of urban residents, by net migration from
the countryside, and by villages or towns expanding to

the point where they become cities or are absorbed by the spread of existing cities.[4]

During the early stages of industrialization, urbanization was largely in response to the pull of employment opportunities in cities. More recently, however, the movement from countryside to city has been more the result of rural push than of urban pull. It is a reflection of the lack of opportunity in the countryside as already small plots of land are divided and then divided again with each passing generation, until they become so small that people can no longer make a living from them.

Historically, cities and the surrounding countryside had a symbiotic relationship, with the latter supplying food and raw materials in exchange for manufactured products. Today cities are tied much more to each other and to the global economy. The food and fuel that once came from the surrounding countryside now often comes from distant corners of the planet.

As societies urbanize, the use of basic resources, such as energy and water, rises. In traditional rural societies, for example, people live on the land and thus do not need to travel to work. But once they migrate to cities, commuting becomes the rule, not the exception. In villages, most of the food that is consumed is produced locally, requiring little energy for processing, packaging, and transportation; once people move into cities, on the other hand, virtually all their food must be brought in. In a village where residents typically draw their water from a central well and carry it to their homes, water use is necessarily limited. But when villagers move to urban high-rise apartment buildings with indoor plumbing, replete with showers and flush toilets, water consumption soars.

The ecology of cities is a continuing challenge to city managers simply because cities require the concentration of huge quantities of water, food, energy, and raw materials. The waste products must then be dispersed or the city will become uninhabitable. As cities become larger, the disposal of residential and industrial wastes becomes ever more challenging.

Partly as a result of the mounting pressure for people to migrate to cities, the growth in urban populations is far outstripping the availability of basic services, such as water, sewerage, transportation, and electricity. As a result, life in urban shantytowns is plagued by poverty, pollution, congestion, homelessness, and unemployment.[5]

Since the beginning of the Industrial Revolution, the terms of trade between countryside and city have favored the latter simply because cities control the scarce resources in development, namely capital and technology. But if the price of food rises in the years ahead, as now seems likely, the terms of trade could shift, favoring the countryside. If in the new world of the twenty-first century the scarce resources are land and water, those controlling them could have the upper hand in determining rural/urban terms of trade.

This aside, if recent trends continue, within the next several years more than half of us will be living in cities—making the world more urban than rural for the first time in history. We will have become an urban species, far removed from our hunter-gatherer origins.

15

Protected Natural Areas

Population growth during the past 50 years has made it difficult to set aside and conserve natural areas. Another half-century of growth will put even more pressure on protected areas as formerly small, distant settlements encroach on these sites and as the number of people (both local and visitors) who use the sites explodes.[1]

National parks, forests, wildlife preserves, beaches, and other protected areas offer sanctuary to various habitats and indigenous communities, in addition to providing resources for local peoples and vital ecosystem services, ranging from erosion control to water filtration. In an urbanizing world, these sites provide an opportunity for healthy interaction with the natural environment, as well as rare serenity.

From Buenos Aires to Bangkok, dramatic urban population growth—and the sprawl and pollution it brings—threatens wilderness areas that lay beyond city limits. Tremendous growth in the population of Bombay has already engulfed Borivili National Park, beyond the city's periphery only a decade ago. With projected growth of 60 percent in the next 20 years, Bombay may soon swallow up more distant areas. On every continent, human encroachment has reduced both the size and the quality of natural areas. (See Table 15–1.)[2]

In nations where rapid population growth has outstripped the carrying capacity of local resources, natural areas become especially vulnerable. Although in industrial nations these areas are synonymous with camping, hiking, and picnics in the country, in Asia, Africa, and Latin America most national parks, forests, and preserves are inhabited or used for natural resources by local populations.[3]

An assessment by the World Conservation Union–IUCN of 30 protected sites in the developing world shows that these areas now act as magnets, attracting people to the rich oasis of water, fuel, food, and other resources they contain. Population growth rates in and around these areas are typically 2 percentage points above the national average—largely as a result of immigration from resource-starved areas.[4]

As people seek out scarce resources, the resulting concentrations can be devastating. For example, population densities in the region surrounding Bwindi Impenetrable National Park in southern Uganda are some of the highest in all of Africa—exceeding 250 people per square kilometer. Though population at this site is expected to multiply, chronic land hunger already precipitates conflicts over fuelwood collection,

TABLE 15–1. *Primary Threats and Conservation Issues, Selected Protected Areas*

Protected Area and Country	Primary Threats and Conservation Issues
Lake Nakuru catchment basin, Kenya	High rates of in-migration contribute to land fragmentation and deforestation around the lake; intensive subsistence farming leads to soil erosion; industrial and domestic effluent from growing Nakuru town; increased tourism.
Jaldapara Wildlife Sanctuary, West Bengal, India	Villagers around the sanctuary are heavily dependent on its resources; villager population doubled from 1971 to 1991 and continues to grow; 25 percent of households are landless and they derive 90 percent of their income from the sanctuary (from sale of firewood, cotton floss, and grass).
Everglades National Park, Florida, United States	Population growth (combined populations of Miami and Fort Lauderdale have grown sevenfold since 1950), soaring water demands, and drainage of wetlands for housing, golf courses, and agricultural expansion threaten the park's health while shrinking its borders.
Royal Bardia National Park, Terai region, Nepal	Population growth (at 3.5 percent annually) inmigration, and tourism contribute to shortages of fuelwood, fodder for livestock, and small timber for construction; this encourages locals to use park resources to meet needs; visitors to the Himalayas have grown from a few hundred in 1970 to 90,000 a year today.

SOURCE: See endnote 2.

farming, cattle grazing, and bush burning.[5]

Migration-driven population growth also endangers wilderness areas in many industrial nations. Everglades National Park, for example, faces collapse as millions of newcomers move into South Florida.[6]

Coastal recreation areas, including beaches, may be

most burdened by the formidable combination of population growth and migration. All but one of the world's 15 largest cities are coastal, and all will grow in the decades ahead. Whether it takes the form of expanding shantytowns in Kingston, Jamaica, or sprawling tract housing in southern California, virtually all the growth and movement in population in the next 50 years will occur in densely populated coastal corridors.[7]

In nations already struggling to meet basic human needs, the prospect of establishing additional protected areas becomes increasingly slim. Throughout India, for example, while the national government designates areas as protected, state and local governments work to de-reserve these sites so that the resources can be harnessed to meet the needs of an additional 18 million Indians each year.[8]

Sunbathers on beaches in Japan are often compared to sardines. People who use Central Park in New York City, which has nearly doubled in population since 1950, are faced with growing congestion and restrictions on activities. National parks throughout North America are confronted with huge backlogs of requests to visit, having to turn tourists away. Tourism at Yosemite has boomed from roughly 4,000 visitors in 1886 to more than 4 million people (and their cars) today. It is often remarked that "Americans love their national parks to death," as increased visitation degrades campsites, trails, and wilderness.[9]

Longer waiting lists and higher user fees for fewer secluded spots are likely the tip of the iceberg, as population growth threatens to eliminate the diversity of habitats and cultures, in addition to the peace and quiet, that protected areas currently house.

16

Education

In contrast to the food supply challenge posed by the coming wave of population growth, the global need for teachers and classrooms will rise very slowly in the next quarter-century, and decline thereafter. This is because the school-age population in many countries is increasing much less rapidly than the overall national population, early evidence of slowing population growth. The trend illustrates that growth rates typically differ for different age strata of the population. It also shows that declining birth rates can take decades to move through an entire population.

At the global level, total population is projected to increase by 47 percent between 2000 and 2050, but the number of children under the age of 15 will actually decline by about 3 percent. (See Figure 16–1.) Indeed,

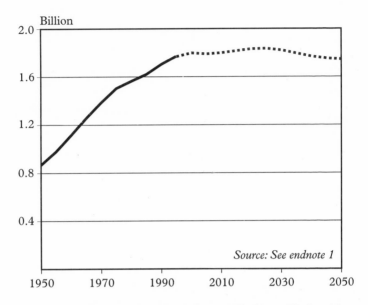

FIGURE 16–1. *World Population of Children Under 15, 1950–95, With Projections to 2050*

most of the world's 10 largest countries will see substantial decreases in child-age population by 2050; for
several of these countries, the decline in this age group
has already begun. (See Table 16–1.) These countries
will need fewer classrooms and teachers to educate the
youngest members of society (assuming they maintain
current class size and student-teacher ratios).[1]

Plenty of nations, however, still have increasing
child-age populations. Where countries have not acted
to stabilize population, the base of the national population pyramid continues to expand, and pressures on the
educational system will be severe. The child-age populations of Niger, Oman, Uganda, and the Democratic
Republic of the Congo will increase by more than 50

Table 16–1. *Children Under 15, Selected Countries,*
2000–2050

Country	Children Under 15		Change in Number of Children Under 15 2000–2050	
	2000	2050		
	(million)		(million)	(percent)
China	317	241	−76	−24
India	338	299	−38	−11
United States	60	60	0	0
Indonesia	65	62	− 3	− 4
Brazil	49	49	0	0
Russia	27	17	− 9	−35
Pakistan	65	75	+10	+15
Japan	19	15	− 4	−23
Bangladesh	45	43	− 2	− 5
Nigeria	48	59	+11	+23

Source: United Nations, *World Population Prospects: The 1998 Revision* (New York: December 1998).

percent by 2050. Africa as a whole will see its child-age population grow by 36 percent through 2030 before it begins to fall.[2]

The rapid growth in African populations is especially worrisome because of the extra burden it imposes in a region already lagging in education. Only 56 percent of Africans south of the Sahara are literate, compared with 71 percent for all developing countries. Few African countries have universal primary education, and secondary education reaches only 4–5 percent of African children. Educating today's children is challenge enough; the addition of another student for every three already there will require heroic investments in education. But the alternative is grim: without additional investment in education, today's average student-teacher ratio of 39 in sub-Saharan Africa will reach 54 by 2040.[3]

Many countries will be challenged to increase funding for education while ensuring that other worthy sectors also receive the support they need. With 900 million illiterate adults in the world, the case for a renewed commitment to education is easy to make. But competing for funds are the 840 million chronically hungry and roughly three billion without access to a decent toilet.[4]

The budget stresses on governments attempting to meet these basic needs would clearly be reduced with smaller populations. Mozambique and Lesotho, for example, both met the UNESCO benchmark for investment in education in 1992—6 percent of gross domestic product—and the two countries' economies were roughly equal in size. Yet because Mozambique has many times the population of Lesotho, spending per child in Lesotho is about nine times higher than in Mozambique. For the majority of countries who do not meet the UNESCO funding standard, many of whom also fall short in providing other basic services, a decline in population pressure could help substantially to meet all of their social goals.[5]

If national education systems begin to stress life-long learning for a rapidly changing world, as recommended by a 1998 UNESCO report on education in the twenty-first century, then extensive provision for adult education will be necessary, affecting even those countries with shrinking child-age populations. Such a development means that countries that started population stabilization programs earliest will be in the best position to educate their entire citizenry.[6]

17

Waste

A growing population increases society's disposal
headaches—the garbage, sewage, and industrial waste
that must be gotten rid of. Even where population is
largely stable—the case in many industrial countries—
the flow of waste products into landfills and waterways
generally continues to increase. Where high rates of
economic and population growth coincide in coming
decades, as they will in many developing countries,
mountains of waste will likely pose difficult disposal
challenges for municipal and national authorities. (See
Table 17–1.)[1]

Data for waste generation in the developing world
are scarce, but citizens in many of these countries are
estimated to produce roughly half a kilo of municipal
waste each day. If this figure is applied to today's pop-

TABLE 17–1. *Challenges for Waste Management in Developing Countries*

Category of Waste	Source of Increased Waste	Disposal Problems
Municipal Solid Waste	Prosperity increases both the weight and volume of waste per person. The average American produces roughly four times as much municipal solid waste as someone in the developing world. Plastic requires more than six times as much volume per unit of weight as food does.	Unless expensive infrastructure is installed, dumps and landfills leach pollutants into groundwater and pose serious health risks to neighbors. They also generate methane, a greenhouse gas. Incinerators can be a serious source of dioxin emissions. And dumping in oceans or other bodies of water creates serious water pollution problems.
Industrial Waste	Industrial waste also increases rapidly as economies prosper. The International Maritime Organization estimated that developing countries produce roughly 6 kilos of hazardous waste per person, but that Eastern Europe generates 50 kilos, and other industrial nations, 100 kilos.	To avoid the hazardous waste legacy of industrial countries, developing nations will need to build special disposal facilities. Yet 45 of 74 countries surveyed by the International Maritime Organization report that hazardous waste is unregulated.
Human and Animal Waste	Human waste grows in step with population, but animal waste may grow more rapidly as prospering countries expand the size of their stocks to meet a growing demand for meat.	Providing adequate sanitation to the unserved half of the world can be very expensive. As livestock raising becomes more centralized, managing animal waste requires capital-intensive facilities, in contrast to the simple waste-to-cropland recycling system long used.

SOURCE: See endnote 1.

ulation, a total of 824 million tons of municipal waste
is being churned out annually in developing countries.
Population growth alone would boost this number to
1.4 billion tons by 2050. But waste rates tend to climb
with rising incomes; a developing world generating as
much waste per capita as industrial countries do today
would be producing some 3.4 billion tons of municipal
waste in 2050. Moreover, prosperity boosts the volume
of waste as the share of plastics, metal, paper, and other
nonorganics rises.[2]

Local and global environmental effects of waste disposal will likely worsen as 2.8 billion people are added
to global population over the next half-century. Acids
from organic wastes, for example, and poisons from
hazardous wastes often leach from landfills, polluting
local groundwater supplies. And rotting organic matter
generates methane, a greenhouse gas. If the waste is
incinerated rather than thrown into landfills, cities will
have to worry about increases in cancer-causing dioxin
emissions, one of the byproducts of burning garbage.

Meanwhile, today's largely unmet sanitation needs
could also be greatly exacerbated by population
growth. Half the world's people do not have access to a
decent toilet, according to UNESCO and the World
Health Organization. Lack of sanitation is a leading
cause of disease: WHO reports that half the developing
world suffers from one of the six diseases associated
with poor water supply and sanitation. One of these,
diarrhea, is the biggest killer of children today, taking
an estimated 2.2 million young lives each year. Unless
the expected growth in population of the developing
world is matched by an increased commitment to provide adequate sanitation, these health problems are
likely to expand.[3]

While the greatest shortage of sanitation is found in rural areas, the need is most urgent in cities, because of the greater potential there for pathogen-tainted water to sicken people on a massive scale. This urban need poses a particular challenge, because the ranks of city dwellers will swell in the next century. In contrast to global population, which is projected to increase by 47 percent over the next half-century, cities will see much greater growth—an estimated 114 percent. Developing-country cities, which failed to meet the sanitation needs of more than a half-billion residents in 1994, will be hard-pressed to service the more than 3 billion people who will be added to cities in the next 50 years.[4]

Prospects for providing access to sanitation are dismal in the near to medium term. Just to keep from losing ground, the rate of provision of service to urban dwellers needs to more than double in Asia. In Africa, it would have to increase by 33 times. And to achieve full coverage by 2020, service provision would have to triple in Asia and increase by 46 times in Africa. Despite the attention focused on sanitation, governments have not demonstrated the will to meet this growing challenge.[5]

18

Conflict

Most environmental security experts agree that population growth alone is rarely the cause of violent conflict. Civil strife tends to be rooted in social disruptions, such as poverty, hunger, ethnopolitical tensions, and government breakdown. Nonetheless, throughout history population growth has worked in tandem with these socioeconomic and political disruptions to drive unstable situations over the edge. At the very least, population growth makes things more precarious.[1]

The steady reduction in per capita local resources, such as fuelwood or cropland, as population grows can become life-threatening in poor rural areas. If no alternate resource supplies exist or if government help is ineffective (or nonexistent), violent conflict may emerge as an attempt to remedy the situation. Today, disputes between rural populations over a shared natural resource are increasingly common in areas as diverse as Central America and southern Africa. (See Table 18–1.)[2]

Population growth has been implicated as an aggravating force in many modern conflicts, ranging from the "soccer war" in central America in 1969 to present-day battles in central Africa. In the 1980s, population-induced land scarcity in Bangladesh led to conflicts that drove more than 10 million refugees into adjacent Indian states. These land-hungry Bengalis in turn exacerbated land shortages in the Indian states—leading to ongoing violent conflict.[3]

Beyond population-driven resource scarcity, the source of deprivation is often structural, related to political, economic, or cultural institutions that perpetuate inequitable access to resources. The process of ecological marginalization—in which large segments of a population are forced into unproductive, ecologically sensitive, or otherwise impoverished settings—can widen the gap between expectations for a better life and actual achievement, heighten civil grievances, and create a situation ripe for conflict.[4]

The concentration of cropland in a few large holdings—on top of population increases—provoked several recent peasant uprisings and land reclamations, including the 1994 Zapatista revolution in Mexico and the Landless Movement currently under way in Brazil by considerably reducing the land available to each household. Without land reform, the projected population increases for Chiapas and Brazil will sharpen scarcity, likely leading to further land seizures and mass squatting.[5]

In the Middle East, a combination of structural and

TABLE 18–1. *Selected Examples of Demographic Conflict Hotspots*

Karachi, Pakistan	Population growth and migration increase numbers in Karachi by 5 percent each year and worsen shortages of jobs, housing, and water for low-income urban dwellers; growing impoverishment aggravates tensions along class, ethnic, and religious lines.
Chiapas, Mexico	Population growth and massive migration from other Mexican states and Guatemala (leading to annual growth of 6 percent) increased pressures on land and drove the bulk of the population onto marginal soils; intensified hunger and poverty increased the likelihood of armed rebellion when opposition groups challenged the local government.
Ningxia province, China (border with Inner Mongolia)	Rapid growth in neighboring herder and farmer populations has driven the availability of a shared water resource well below subsistence level; in recent drought years, gangs of farmers have begun to raid the land of neighboring herders, stealing forage crops for food.
Rwanda	Decades of rapid population growth leading to severe water and land scarcity, declining soil fertility, and extensive deforestation by 1994 created a nation of impoverished, restless citizens easily driven by opposition parties to violence once government breakdown eliminated nonviolent response channels.

SOURCE: See endnote 2.

demographic-driven water scarcity has fed other long-standing tensions. For example, water scarcity in Gaza—at the root of conflicts between Israelis and Palestinians—results from rapid population growth in the Gaza strip and neighboring nations, pollution and depletion of aquifer waters, and inequitable distribution of water between Palestinian and Israeli communities. Disputes in the Nile River Basin between Egypt and Ethiopia, in the Colorado Basin between the United States and Mexico, and in the Mekong Basin between Viet Nam and Thailand are rooted simultaneously in demographic and distributional factors.[6]

As rural population growth decreases the possibility of eking out a decent living, the effects of scarcity can spill over to the city through massive rural-urban migrations. At stake in the urban environment is not only scarcity of natural resources, but shortages of infrastructure, housing, and jobs, leading to poverty, unemployment, and social unrest. From Los Angeles to Lagos, swelling populations hamper provision of basic social services to poor city dwellers, creating a volatile setting if food shortages or economic recession suddenly worsen the situation.[7]

It is increasingly clear that population-induced conflicts can quickly spill beyond a nation's borders in many well-known—though unpredictable—ways, such as massive outflows of refugees, creation of humanitarian emergencies, and seizure of border areas by warring parties. Thomas Homer-Dixon of the University of Toronto calls attention to several pivotal nations whose stability profoundly affects regional and global security, and who are at risk of demographic-related conflict, including South Africa, Mexico, Pakistan, India, and China.[8]

Whether induced by population growth or unfair distribution, resource scarcity currently affects a majority of the population in many developing countries. Continued population growth can only worsen the situation, increasing the number of people who face scarcity and subsequently the number for whom this will serve as justification for rebellion.

19

Meat Production

World meat production increased from 44 million tons in 1950 to 216 million tons in 1998, expanding almost twice as fast as population. In per capita terms, world meat production expanded from 17 kilograms in 1950 to over 36 kilograms in 1998, more than doubling. (See Figure 19–1.) Growth in meat production was originally concentrated in western industrial countries and Japan, but over the last two decades it has increased rapidly in East Asia (especially China), the Middle East, and Latin America.[1]

When incomes begin to rise in traditional low-income societies, one of the first things people do is diversify their diets, consuming more livestock products. People everywhere appear to have an innate desire to consume at least moderate quantities of meat, per-

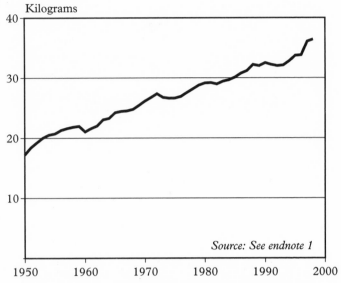

FIGURE 19–1. *World Meat Production Per Person,*
1950–98

haps reflecting our evolutionary history as hunter-gatherers.

Three types of meat—beef, pork, and poultry—account for the bulk of world consumption; mutton ranks a distant fourth. From 1950 until 1980, beef and pork production followed the same trend, but after the economic reforms in China—where pork is dominant—pork production surged ahead, climbing from 45 million tons to 90 million tons in less than two decades.[2]

Historically, growth in the world meat supply came primarily from beef and mutton, sustained by the world's rangelands. These areas, consisting mostly of land that is too arid to support crop production, cover a vast part of the planet, roughly double the cropland area. Not only do the herds of cattle and flocks of sheep and goats provide meat and milk, but for millions of people in Africa, the Middle East, Central Asia, parts of the Indian subcontinent, and western China, they provide a livelihood. The only feasible way that this land can contribute to the world's food supply is to graze cattle, sheep, and goats on it, producing the meat and milk that directly and indirectly sustain a large segment of humanity.

In recent years, beef and mutton production have leveled off at just over 60 million tons per year as the number of animals has pressed against the carrying capacity of rangelands. With little unused grazing capacity left, future gains in meat production will have to come largely from feeding animals grain. At this point, the relative conversion efficiency of various animals begins to influence production trends. Producing a kilogram of beef in the feedlot requires roughly seven kilograms of grain, while a kilogram of pork requires nearly four of grain and a kilogram of poultry, just over two. As grain supplies tighten, the advantage shifts from beef to pork and even more so to poultry. This helps explain why world poultry production overtook that of beef in 1995.[3]

Of the world grain harvest of 1.85 billion tons in 1998, a full 36 percent—or nearly 700 million tons—will be used to feed livestock and poultry, producing milk and eggs as well as meat. This share, remarkably stable for the last decade, could go up or down depending on future grain prices.[4]

Expanding world meat production also depends on soybean production. If the grain fed to livestock or poultry is supplemented with a modest amount of soybean meal (the high protein meal that is left after the oil is extracted), its conversion into meat is much more efficient. Largely as a result of this growing demand for livestock products, world soybean production climbed from 17 million tons in 1950 to 154 million tons in 1998, a gain of ninefold.[5]

To project the future demand for meat, we assume that the growth in meat consumption per person will slow over the next half-century, rising by one half instead of doubling, since some countries are nearing the saturation point. This, combined with the projected growth in population, would push total meat consumption from 216 million tons in 1998 to 481 million tons in 2050, a gain of 265 million tons. If we assume an average of 3 kilograms of grain per kilogram of meat produced, this would require nearly 800 million tons of additional grain for feed in 2050, an amount equal to half of current world grain consumption. This would greatly intensify the competition between grain consumed directly and that consumed indirectly as animal protein, calling into question whether such gains in meat consumption will ever materialize.[6]

Grain fed to livestock and poultry is now the principal food reserve in the event of a world food emergency. As of 1990, the world had, in effect, three reserves in the global food system: substantial stocks of grain that could be drawn upon in the event of unexpected shortages, a large area of cropland idled under U.S. farm commodity programs, and grain fed to animals. By 1998, world grain stocks had been depleted to one of the lowest levels on record and the cropland that was idled for half a century was returned to production. The only safety net remaining in the event of a major crop failure is the grain fed to livestock and poultry.[7]

20

Income

Global economic output, the total of all goods and services produced, grew from $6 trillion in 1950 to $39 trillion in 1998, expanding nearly three times faster than population. This increase of nearly sevenfold boosted incomes rather substantially for most of humanity. It also created a huge economy, one whose growth from 1990 to 1998 exceeded the growth during the 10,000 years from the beginning of agriculture until 1950.[1]

In per capita terms, economic output climbed from just over $2,500 in 1950 to over $6,600 in 1998, a gain of 164 percent. (See Figure 20–1.) Although there is an enormous income gap between industrial and developing countries, the latter's economies are growing far more rapidly. Growth in industrial countries has slowed

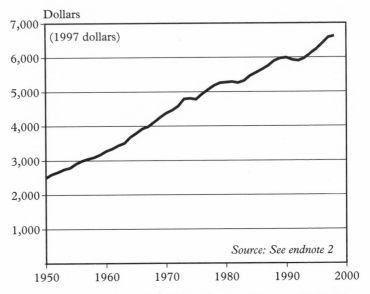

FIGURE 20–1. *Gross World Product Per Person, 1950–98*

to scarcely 2 percent a year during the 1990s, compared with nearly 6 percent a year in developing nations.[2]

The fastest-growing region in the world from 1990 to 1997 was Asia, which averaged nearly 8 percent annually. This growth was led by China, whose economy has been increasing at nearly 10 percent a year throughout much of this decade, making it the world's fastest-growing economy. Since 1980, China's economic output has doubled every eight years.[3]

Incomes have risen most rapidly in developing countries where population growth has slowed the most, including, importantly, the countries of East Asia—South Korea, Taiwan, China, Thailand, Indonesia, and Malaysia. Concentrating early on reducing birth rates helped to boost savings to invest in education, health care, and the infrastructure needed by a modern industrial society.[4]

At the other end of the spectrum, African countries—largely ignoring family planning—have been overwhelmed by the sheer numbers of young people who need to be educated and employed. With population growth rates remaining at close to 3 percent or more a year, most of any economic growth that occurred has been absorbed by the increasing population, leaving little to raise incomes.[5]

The enormous growth during the 1990s, particularly in East Asia, is due to the huge increase in private capital flows into developing countries. Between 1990 and 1997, annual private capital flows increased from $42 billion to $256 billion, a gain of more than sixfold. This substantial amount of money dwarfs traditional flows in public funds under international aid programs.[6]

Although incomes in much of the developing world are rising rapidly, they are not rising for everyone. The World Bank estimates that 1.3 billion of the world's people subsist on $1 a day or less. For this one fifth of humanity, trapped at a subhuman level of existence, there has not been any meaningful progress.[7]

The sources of growth are changing. In earlier times, most of the growth was in agriculture. Since the advent of the Industrial Revolution, however, more and more of the growth has been concentrated in industry. Then beginning around mid-century, the services sector—insurance, banking, education—began to expand rapidly, accounting for most of the change in the industrial world. More recently, growth has been concentrated in the information sector as computerization of the economy and telecommunications have grown at extraordinary rates.

The good news is that the global economy has been expanding at a near record pace during the 1990s. The bad news is that the economy, as now structured, is outgrowing the Earth's ecosystem. The sevenfold growth in the global economy since 1950 has created a huge economy, one that is putting excessive pressures on natural systems and resources. As noted in Chapter 1, from 1950 to 1998 the use of fuelwood more than doubled. That of paper increased sixfold, the fish catch increased nearly fivefold, grain consumption nearly tripled, fossil fuel burning nearly quadrupled, and air and water pollutants multiplied severalfold. The unfortunate reality is that the economy continues to expand, but the ecosystem on which it depends does not, creating an increasingly stressed relationship.[8]

If the economy were to expand only enough to cover population growth until 2050, it would need to grow from the $39 trillion of 1998 to $59 trillion. This, of course, would merely maintain current incomes, unacceptable though they are for much of humanity. If, on the other hand, the economy were to continue to expand at 3 percent per year, global economic output would reach $183 trillion in the year 2050.

Even the first, more modest, growth projection would likely lead to a deterioration of the Earth's natural systems to the point where the economy itself would begin to decline. It is easy to foresee a scenario of continuing forest destruction, aquifer depletion, and ecosystem collapse that would lead to economic decline. If the world cannot simultaneously convert the economy to one that is environmentally sustainable—one that does not destroy its own support systems—and move to a lower population trajectory, economic decline will be hard to avoid.

II

Conclusion

21

The Emergence of Demographic Fatigue

As noted in Chapter 1, the demographic prospect for individual countries has never varied more widely than it does today. In some industrial nations, populations are already stable and are projected to decline somewhat over the next half-century, while in others they are projected to more than triple. But are such increases realistic? The preceding analysis of 19 dimensions of the population problem raises doubts as to whether the expected population doublings and triplings in scores of developing countries will in fact materialize.

There is no precedent by which to judge the effects of the population growth rates of 3 percent a year, which leads to a 20-fold increase in a century. Until the middle of this century, no country had experienced the sustained 3-percent growth that has been posted in scores of developing countries since then. Now with several decades of rapid population growth behind us, we can begin to see some of the effects of such growth. It comes as no surprise that governments in many countries that have experienced rapid growth for nearly two generations are showing signs of demographic fatigue. Worn down by the struggle to deal with the consequences of rapid population growth, they are unable to respond to new threats, such as AIDS, aquifer depletion, and the flooding that can follow deforestation.

Problems routinely managed in industrial societies are becoming full-scale humanitarian crises in many developing ones. As a result, some developing countries with rapidly growing populations that were until recently headed for a doubling of their populations are now looking at population stability, or even population decline—not because of falling birth rates, but because of rapidly rising death rates. This reversal in the death rate trend marks a tragic new development in world demography. In the absence of a concerted effort by national governments and the international community to quickly shift to smaller families, events in many countries could spiral out of control, leading to spreading political instability and economic decline.

★   ★   ★   ★

To help assess the likelihood that the increases projected by the United Nations will actually occur, we turn to the concept of the demographic transition, formulated by Princeton demographer Frank Notestein in 1945. Among other things, its three stages help explain widely disparate population growth rates. In the first stage, which prevails in preindustrial societies, birth rates and death rates are both high, essentially offsetting each other and leading to little or no population growth. As countries begin to modernize, however, death rates fall and countries enter stage two, where death rates are low while birth rates remain high. At this point, population growth typically reaches 3 percent a year. Countries cannot remain in this stage long.[1]

As modernization continues, birth rates fall and countries enter the third and final stage of the demographic transition, when birth rates and death rates again balance, but at low levels. At this point, population size stabilizes. Countries rarely ever have exactly zero growth, but here we consider any country with annual growth below 0.4 percent to have an essentially stable population. Among the earliest nations to reach stage three were East Germany, West Germany, Hungary, and Sweden, which achieved stability during the 1970s.

All countries today are in either stage two or stage three. As noted in Chapter 1, some 32 industrial countries have made it to stage three, stabilizing their population size. (See Table 21–1.) The other 160 or so countries, including most of those in Asia, Africa, and Latin America, are in stage two. Within this group 39 countries, those that have seen their fertility fall to replacement level or below, are approaching stage three. Included here are China and the United States, which are each growing by roughly 1 percent a year.[2]

In mature industrial countries with stable populations, agricultural claims on the Earth's ecosystem are beginning to level off. In the European Union (EU), for example, population has stabilized at roughly 380 million. With incomes already high, grain consumption per

TABLE 21–1. *Sixteen Countries with Zero Population Growth, 1998[1]*

Country	Annual Rate of Natural Increase (percent)	Midyear Population (million)
Belarus	−0.4	10
Belgium	+0.1	10
Czech Republic	−0.2	10
France	+0.3	59
Germany	−0.1	82
Greece	0	10
Hungary	−0.4	10
Italy	0	58
Japan	+0.2	126
Netherlands	+0.3	16
Poland	+0.1	39
Romania	−0.2	22
Russia	−0.5	147
Spain	0	39
Ukraine	−0.6	50
United Kingdom	+0.2	59

[1]Includes only the larger countries, those with 10 million or more people.
SOURCE: Population Reference Bureau, "1998 World Population Data Sheet," wall chart (Washington DC: June 1998).

person has plateaued at around 470 kilograms a year. As a result, EU member countries, consuming roughly 180 million tons of grain annually, have essentially stabilized their claims on the Earth's agricultural resources—the first region in the world to do so. (See Figure 21–1.)[3]

And, perhaps more important, since the region is a net exporter of grain, Europe has done this within the limits of its own land and water resources. Likewise, future demand for grain in both North America and Eastern Europe is also projected to remain within the

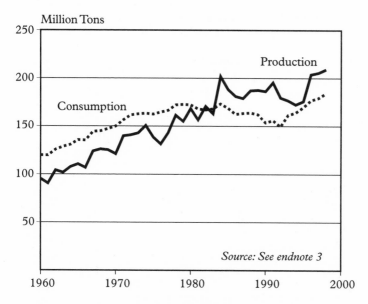

FIGURE 21–1. *Grain Consumption in the European Union, 1960–1998*

carrying capacity of regional land and water resources.[4]

Not all countries are so fortunate. Over the next half-century, India's population is projected to overtake that of China, as it expands by 540 million people, compared with 235 million for China. Whether India—already facing acute shortages of water—can avoid a breakdown of social systems in the face of such a rise in population pressure remains to be seen.

Although there are dozens of countries that now face a projected doubling or tripling of population size over the next half-century, three of the more populous ones stand out: Ethiopia, Nigeria, and Pakistan. (See Table 21–2.) The current fertility rate in these countries ranges from just under six children per woman in Pak-

TABLE 21–2. *Population in Selected Industrial and Developing Countries in 1998, With Projections to 2050*

Area	Population 1998	2050	Increase From 1998 to 2050 (million)	(percent)
	(million)		(million)	(percent)
Industrial Countries				
United States	270	349	+79	+29
Russia	147	121	−26	−18
Japan	126	105	−21	−17
Germany	82	73	− 9	−11
France	59	60	+ 1	+ 2
United Kingdom	58	57	− 1	− 2
Italy	57	41	−16	−28
Developing Countries				
India	989	1,529	+540	+ 55
China	1,243	1,478	+235	+ 19
Pakistan	142	345	+203	+143
Nigeria	122	244	+122	+100
Brazil	162	244	+ 82	+ 51
Bangladesh	123	212	+ 89	+ 72
Ethiopia	58	169	+111	+191
Congo	49	160	+ 111	+227
Mexico	98	147	+ 49	+ 50
Iran	64	115	+ 51	+ 80
Egypt	66	115	+ 49	+ 74
Tanzania	31	81	+ 50	+161

SOURCE: Population Reference Bureau, "1998 World Population Data Sheet," wall chart (Washington DC: June 1998); United Nations, *World Population Prospects: The 1998 Revision* (New York: December 1998).

istan to nearly seven in Ethiopia. By 2050, water availability per person in each of these countries will be well below the minimum needed to satisfy basic food and residential needs.[5]

In addition, there are many smaller countries that are facing potentially overwhelming population growth. Among them are the Congo, going from 49 million today to 160 million in 2050; Tanzania, going from 31 million to 81 million; and Yemen, going from 17 million to 59 million. The latter two are already facing crippling water shortages.

The question now facing the world is whether the 160 or so countries that are still in stage two, with continuing population growth, can make it into stage three by quickly reducing births. Over the next half-century, most countries where population growth is still substantial seem likely to break out of stage two, achieving the demographic stability of stage three. In these nations, the combination of falling fertility, rising incomes, and rising educational levels will lead to population stabilization within the foreseeable future. Economic and social gains and the decline in fertility will reinforce each other.

This can be seen most clearly in the developing countries of East Asia, such as South Korea and Taiwan, where successful early efforts to reduce fertility set the stage for the diversion of capital from rearing large numbers of children to investment in modernization and the overall improvement of living conditions. As the number of children per couple declined, so too did dependency ratios—the proportion of the non-working dependent population, primarily children, to the working-age population—easing the financial burden of supporting these dependents. The freeing of funds allowed increased savings rates and investment, leading ultimately to enhanced productivity, strong economic growth, and rising incomes. The resulting improvements in living standards then reinforced the trend to smaller families.[6]

Countries that are already pressing against the limits of land and water resources and that are faced with a projected doubling or tripling of their population may face falling living standards that will further reinforce the prevailing high fertility. This reinforcing mechanism, referred to by demographers as the demographic trap, could keep living standards at the subsistence level, and eventually lead to rising mortality as the land and water resource base deteriorates, driving countries back into stage one.

Nations in stage two where population is still growing rapidly will thus either shift quickly to smaller families and advance to stage three or eventually fall back into stage one of the demographic transition when their economic and social systems break down under mounting population pressure. One or the other of the two self-reinforcing cycles will take over. There are no other options. Among the many countries at risk of falling back into stage one if they do not quickly check their population growth are Afghanistan, Egypt, Ethiopia, Ghana, Haiti, Honduras, India, Myanmar, Nigeria, Pakistan, the Sudan, Tanzania, and Yemen.

Governments of countries that have been in stage two for several decades are typically worn down and drained of financial resources by the consequences of rapid population growth, in effect suffering from demographic fatigue. This includes trying to educate ever growing numbers of children reaching school age, creating jobs for the swelling numbers of young people entering the job market, and dealing with the various environmental problems associated with rapid population growth, such as deforestation, increased flooding, soil erosion, and aquifer depletion.

With leadership and fiscal resources stretched thin in trying to cope with so many pressures at once, governments are often unable to respond effectively to emerging threats such as water shortages or food shortages. This is perhaps most evident in the inability of many governments to cope with new diseases, such as AIDS, or the resurgence of more traditional ones, such as malaria or tuberculosis.

If these threats are not dealt with, they can force countries back into stage one. For several African countries with high HIV infection levels, this is no longer a hypothetical prospect. Although industrial nations have been able to control the spread of the disease, holding infection levels under 1 percent of their populations, governments in many developing countries—already overwhelmed by the pressures just described—have not been able to do so.

For example, in Zimbabwe—a country of 11 million people—more than 1.4 million of the adult population of less than 5.6 million are infected with HIV. As a result of this 26-percent adult infection rate and the inability to pay for costly drugs needed to treat those with the disease, Zimbabwe is expected to reach population stability in 2002 as death rates climb to offset birth rates. In effect, it will have fallen back into stage one, marking perhaps the first time that a developing country has reached population stability primarily as a result of rising death rates.[7]

In contrast to most potentially fatal diseases, AIDS takes its toll not so much among the very young and the elderly, but among the young professionals in the prime of life—the very agronomists, engineers, and teachers needed to develop the economy. Again, using Zimbabwe to illustrate, life expectancy—perhaps the sentinel indicator of a society's health—is expected to drop from 61 years in 1993 to 49 in 2000 and, if the recent rise in infections continues, to 40 in 2010. Measured by this key social indicator, this represents a reversal of development, turning it back a half-century or more. These trends are more reminiscent of the Dark Ages than the bright new millennium that many had hoped for.[8]

Other African countries that are also expected to soon reach zero population growth as rising death rates offset high fertility are Botswana (an HIV adult infection rate of 25 percent), Namibia (20 percent), Zambia (19 percent), and Swaziland (18 percent). Other nations where roughly 1 out of 10 adults is now infected with the virus and where the HIV/AIDS epidemic is spiraling out of control include Burundi, the Central African Republic, the Congo, Côte d'Ivoire, Ethiopia, Kenya, Malawi, Mozambique, Rwanda, South Africa, and Tanzania. In the absence of a concerted effort to check the spread of the virus, these countries too are heading for a rise in death rates that will bring their population growth to a halt.[9]

Unfortunately, the HIV epidemic is also spreading in Asia and Latin America. An estimated 4 million Indians, or about 1 percent of the adult population, are HIV-positive. In Latin America, Haiti tops the list, with 5 percent of its population testing positive, while Brazil, which has the largest number of infected adults at 570,000, is still under 1 percent.[10]

There is no recent historical example for an infectious disease threatening to take so many lives as the HIV epidemic. To find a precedent for such a potentially devastating loss of life from an infectious disease, we have to go back to the decimation of New World Indian communities by the introduction of smallpox in the sixteenth century or to the bubonic plague that claimed roughly a fourth of Europe's population during the fourteenth century. (See Table 21–3.) The HIV epidemic should be seen for what it is—an epidemic of epic proportions that, if not checked soon, could claim more lives during the early part of the twenty-first century than World War II did during the twentieth century.[11]

Another situation that could easily become unmanageable is life-threatening shortages of food due to either land or water shortages or both. For example, Pakistan and Nigeria face an impossible challenge in trying to feed their future populations as their cropland per person promises to shrink below the survival level. The projected growth for Pakistan to 345 million by 2050 will reduce its grainland per person from 0.08 hectares at present to 0.03 hectares, roughly the strip between the 10-yard markers on a football field. Nigeria's projected growth will reduce its grainland per person from the currently inadequate 0.15 hectares to 0.07 hectares.[12]

As India's population approaches the 1 billion mark and as it faces the addition of another 500 million people by 2050, it must deal with steep cutbacks in irrigation water. David Seckler, head of the International Water Management Institute in Sri Lanka, the world's premier water research body, observes in a new study that "the extraction of water from aquifers in India exceeds recharge by a factor of 2 or more. Thus almost everywhere in India, fresh-water aquifers are being pulled down by 1–3 meters per year."[13]

Seckler goes on to speculate that as aquifers are depleted, the resulting cutbacks in irrigation could reduce India's harvest by 25 percent. In a country where food supply and demand are precariously balanced and where 18 million people are added to the population each year, the cutbacks in irrigation that are

TABLE 21–3. *Profiles of Major Epidemics Throughout Human History*

Epidemic and Date	Mode of Introduction and Spread	Description of Plague and Its Effects on Population
Black Death in Europe, 14th century	Originating in Asia, the plague bacteria moved westward via trade routes, entering Europe in 1347; transmitted via rats as well as coughing and sneezing.	One fourth of the population of Europe was wiped out (an estimated 25 million deaths); old, young, and poor hit hardest.
Smallpox in the New World, 16th century	Spanish conquistadors and European colonists introduced virus into the Americas, where it spread through respiratory channels and physical contact.	Decimated Incan, Aztec, and native North American civilizations, killing 10–20 million.
Influenza, worldwide, 1918–19	American World War I troops probably brought virus back from Europe; virus spread quickly along transport routes to entire world; transmitted through respiratory channels.	25–40 million deaths worldwide (1.3–2.2 percent of population); 12.5 million in India; 550,000 in the United States (0.5 percent of population); old, young, and poor most affected.
HIV/AIDS, worldwide, 1980 to present	Thought to have originated in Africa; a primate virus that mutated spread to infect humans; transmitted by the exchange of bodily fluids, including blood, semen, and breast milk.	More than 12 million deaths worldwide thus far; 30 million (0.5% percent of the world) infected; one fifth of adult population infected in several African nations; strikes economically active population hardest.

SOURCE: See endnote 11.

in prospect could drop food supplies below the survival level, creating a national food emergency.[14]

As noted earlier, U.N. demographic projections do not reflect the ecological deterioration and social breakdown of the sort that has led to the ethnic conflicts plaguing countries such as Rwanda and Somalia. Somalia, for example, is still treated by U.N. demographers as a country, but in reality it is not. It is a geographic area inhabited by warring clans—one where ongoing conflict, disintegration of health care services, and widespread hunger combine to raise mortality.

Exactly how the stresses of social disintegration will manifest themselves as the needs of a growing population outstrip the resource base varies from country to country. For example, Rwanda's 1950 population of 2.5 million had reached roughly 8.5 million by early 1994. A country whose agricultural development was once cited as a model for others in Africa saw its grainland area per person shrink to a meager 0.03 hectares per person, less than one third as much as in Bangladesh, one of the world's more land-scarce countries.[15]

In this society, which is almost entirely rural with no industrial cities to migrate to, cropland per person has shrunk to the point where it will no longer adequately feed many of those living on the land, giving rise to a quiet desperation. The resulting tension can easily be ignited—as it was when an age-old ethnic conflict between Tutsis and Hutus broke out again in 1994, leading to the slaughter of a half-million Rwandans, mostly Tutsis.[16]

The press focused on the long-standing conflict, which was real, but what was not reported was the extraordinary population growth over the last half-century and how it was affecting the hope of Rwandans for a better future. Desperate people resort to desperate actions.

★   ★   ★   ★

The issues discussed here raise several complex questions. For example, what is the psychological effect on a society that loses a substantial share of its adult population in a matter of years? What happens when aquifer depletion starts shrinking the food supply in countries with fast-growing populations? Will governments that have permitted AIDS to decimate their populations or that have allowed aquifers to be depleted lose their legitimacy and be voted out or overthrown? No one knows the answer to these questions because continuing population growth and the problems it eventually generates are taking the world into uncharted territory.

As demographic fatigue sets in and the inability of governments to deal effectively with the consequences of rapid population growth becomes more evident, the resulting social stresses are likely to exacerbate conflicts among differing religious, ethnic, tribal, or geographic groups within societies. Among these are differences between Hindus and Moslems in India; Yorubas, Ibos, and Hausas in Nigeria; Arabs and Israelis in the Middle East; Hutus and Tutsis in Rwanda and Burundi; and many others. Aside from enormous social costs, these spreading conflicts could drive countless millions across national borders as they seek safety, putting pressure on industrial countries to admit them as political refugees.

As pressures on the Earth's resources build, they may also lead to international conflicts over shared water resources, oceanic fisheries, or other scarce resources. Nowhere is the potential conflict over scarce water more stark than among the three principal countries of the Nile River valley—Egypt, the Sudan, and Ethiopia. In Egypt, where it rarely rains, agriculture is almost wholly dependent on water from the Nile. Egypt now gets the lion's share of the Nile's water, but its current population of 66 million is projected to reach 115 million by 2050, thus greatly boosting the demand for grain, even without any gains in per capita consumption.

The Sudan, whose population is projected to double from 29 million today to 59 million by 2050, also depends heavily on the Nile. The population of Ethiopia, the country that controls 85 percent of the headwaters of the Nile, is projected to expand from 58 million to 169 million. With little Nile water now reaching the Mediterranean, if either of the two upstream countries, Sudan or Ethiopia, use more water, Egypt will get less.[17]

After the political situation stabilized in Ethiopia, national attention turned to economic development and the government built 200 small dams. Although these are collectively taking only 500 million cubic meters of water out of the Nile's total flow of 85 billion cubic meters, the government plans to use much more of the Nile's water as it expands power generation and irrigation in the effort to lift its people out of poverty.[18]

With gross national product per person in Ethiopia averaging only $100 per year compared with $1,080 in Egypt, it is difficult to argue that the former should not use more of the Nile's water. As the collective population of these three countries expands by 190 million, going from 153 million at present to 343 million in 2050, it is simply outstripping the local supply of water. Although it is only one of the many potential conflicts that could be triggered as population pressures mount, this one—involving both Muslims and Christians—could destabilize the entire Middle East.[19]

The adverse effects of population growth will affect citizens in seemingly far removed nations, such as the United States or Germany, as globalization increasingly defines national economies and domestic welfare. As economist Herman Daly observes, whereas in the past surplus labor in one nation had the effect of driving down wages only in that nation, "global economic integration will be the means by which the consequences of overpopulation in the Third World are generalized to the globe as a whole." Large infusions into Brazil's or India's work force that may lower wages in those nations mean large infusions into the global work force with potentially similar consequences.[20]

As the recent Asian economic downturn further demonstrates, "localized instability" is becoming an anachronistic concept. The consequences of social unrest in one nation, whether resulting from a currency crisis or an environmental crisis, can quickly cross national boundaries. Several nations, including the United States, now recognize world population growth as a national security issue with economic, environmental, and military consequences. As the U.S. Department of State Strategic Plan, issued in September 1997, explains, "Stabilizing population growth is vital to U.S. interests....Not only will early stabilization of the world's population promote environmentally sustainable economic development in other countries, but it will benefit the U.S. by improving trade opportunities and mitigating future global crises."[21]

★   ★   ★   ★

As we look to the future, the challenge for world leaders is to help countries maximize the prospects for breaking out of stage two of the demographic transition and moving into stage three before demographic fatigue takes over and nature brutally forces them back into stage one.

In a world where both grain output and fish catch per person are falling, a strong case can be made on humanitarian grounds for an all-out effort to stabilize world population. There is nothing inevitable about a projected mid-century population of 8.9 billion. We can choose to move to the lower trajectory of the three U.N. projection scenarios, which has world population stabilizing at 7.3 billion by 2050. (See Figure 21–2.) This would reduce the number to be added by 2050 from 2.8 billion to a more manageable 1.3 billion.[22]

What is needed, to use a basketball term, is a full-court press—an all-out effort to lower fertility, particularly in high-fertility countries, before demographic fatigue takes over, leading to higher mortality and forcing countries back into stage one of the demographic transition. We see two parts to this effort: national carrying capacity assessments to help governments and the public at large to better understand the urgency of stabilizing population, and national population programs that bring population growth rates under control by emphasizing the empowerment of women, strengthening health care, and promoting family planning.

Two hundred years ago, Thomas Malthus advanced humanity's understanding of carrying capacity through his insights into the population-food supply relationship. Today, our understanding of carrying capacity encompasses many of the dimensions discussed in this book, and the tools used are far more sophisticated.

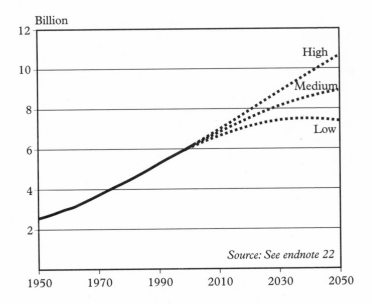

FIGURE 21–2. *World Population Projections Under Three Variants, 1950–2050*

Malthus would be astonished at the variables used in today's analyses of carrying capacity with regard to food.

We know, for example, what every country's cropland area is and roughly what it will be a half-century from now. Current hydrological data give us a good sense of how much water will be available for each country in 2050, assuming no major changes in climate. And we know that annual increases in yields—the engine of growth in world food production over the past 50 years—will likely continue to slow, as crop yields in more countries push up against physiological limits.[23]

With this information, governments can calculate

their population carrying capacity for food, and assess their population policy in light of the results. And they can do similar analyses of their country's need for materials, energy, waste absorption, and other dimensions of carrying capacity.

Governments may assume they can cover shortfalls in future needs with imports. But this may not be realistic, as the case of agriculture again demonstrates. The projected growth in national grain deficits worldwide at current prices is collectively likely to far exceed exportable grain surpluses, which have increased little since 1980. (See Figure 21–3.) Although exports from only four countries and the European Union are included in Figure 21–3, they account for easily four fifths of the global total. Even though the cropland held out of production under U.S. farm commodity programs over the last half-century was returned to use after these programs were dismantled in 1995, the United States—the world's leading grain exporter—has actually experienced some shrinkage in its exportable surplus in recent years as the growth in domestic demand has exceeded the growth in production.[24]

Nations that assume they can turn to international markets indefinitely for grain might reassess their outlook once they complete an assessment of carrying capacity—and once they study those of other countries and assess their collective import needs.

Given the limits to the carrying capacity of each country's natural resources, every government now needs a carefully articulated and adequately supported population policy, one that takes into account the country's carrying capacity at whatever consumption level citizens decide on. As Harvard biologist Edward O. Wilson observes in his landmark book *The Diversity*

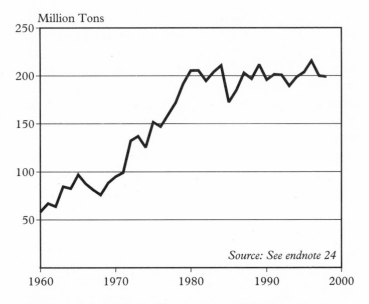

FIGURE 21–3. *Grain Exports from Argentina, Canda, European Union, and the United States, 1960–98*

of Life, "Every nation has an economic policy and a foreign policy. The time has come to speak more openly of a population policy. By this I mean not just the capping of growth when the population hits the wall, as in China and India, but a policy based on a rational solution of this problem; what, in the judgment of its informed citizenry, is the optimal population?"[25]

Once the urgency of the population challenge becomes apparent to governments and citizens, population programs—the second part of the equation—form the backbone of a national population policy by offering the means to reduce fertility rates and stabilize population.

Decades of population assistance efforts throughout

the world have demonstrated that fertility decline is a dynamic process with multiple forces acting as both cause and consequence. Increased availability and awareness of contraception, improved literacy rates, reduced infant mortality, and better economic prospects all typically drive declines in fertility. Fertility reductions, in turn, reinforce these factors in positive feedback cycles. The more of these factors that are present, the more likely that the transition to lower fertility will be rapid, widespread, and sustained.

The transition to lower fertility rates is enhanced by altering the gender structure of society—affording women the same educational, political, and economic opportunities available to men. In every society for which data are available, the more education women have, the fewer children they have. In Egypt, for example, 56 percent of women with no schooling became mothers while still in their teens, compared with just 5 percent of women who remained in school past the primary level.[26]

Women often delay marriage and having children— reducing the total number of children they ultimately bear—because they wish to finish their formal education. School serves as an opportunity to venture beyond the social mores that persist in the traditional family setting, thus changing women's aspirations and values, as well as instilling the confidence to break from the norm.

Increased economic and political opportunities— including the basic rights to vote, own land and other property, and hold a job—broaden the lifestyle choices available to women while providing the autonomy to determine their own reproductive destiny. Recent efforts to couple family planning programs with microlending, jobs skills training, and other attempts to boost female economic prospects have been able to take advantage of the synergies derived from providing women with both contraception and a means to boost social standing. Increased economic opportunities for both men and women reduce the emphasis on a large family as a source of future financial security.[27]

Gains in maternal and child health care, and subsequent reductions in mortality, give couples additional power to control the number of children they ultimately have. Where infant and child mortality rates are high, couples may have large families for fear of losing some of their children. China's "barefoot doctor" campaign, which helped cut infant mortality rates from 195 deaths per 1,000 life births in 1955 to just 40 today, was instrumental in the rapid fertility reduction over the same period.[28]

Once the number of children a couple desires has been reduced, the primary tool for reaching this number is family planning, which encompasses reproductive health services, contraception, and counseling on fertility control choices. Unfortunately, there currently exists a substantial unmet need for family planning—the gap between desired and actual fertility.

In developing nations, this unmet need confronts 10–40 percent of married women of reproductive age—and a large but unknown number of unmarried women. A substantial portion of the world's pregnancies remain unintended and unwanted, even as the number of people coming of reproductive age nears its highest level ever. As more couples desire smaller families, this unmet need will swell without stepped-up family planning efforts.[29]

Beyond the many maternal and child health benefits

of family planning, there is now another powerful reason for filling this family planning gap: the HIV epidemic. The same family planning network—the same counselors on sexually transmitted diseases and fertility control options—can provide the grassroots foundation for checking the spread of HIV. The same condoms that limit fertility can also limit the spread of the virus.

The simultaneous occurrence of rapid population growth and rampant HIV infection in many nations is symptomatic of the same underlying social problems. From Somalia to Cambodia, inadequate public provision of education and health services—including contraception—are at the root of continuing rapid population growth and the spread of the HIV virus. To be successful, both population programs and HIV prevention campaigns depend on reducing the share of the population that lacks these basic social entitlements.

Worldwide, the transition to lower fertility—with related changes in gender equality, personal aspirations, and access to family planning—has occurred at diverse socioeconomic levels, including widely disparate rates of infant mortality, female school enrollment, and urbanization. When fertility rates began to decline in Mexico in the mid-1970s, for example, incomes were well above the developing-nation average, infant mortality was well below the average, and most people lived in cities. In contrast, in Bangladesh the fertility decline began in the early 1970s with average income at a fraction of the Mexican level, several times the infant mortality, and just 10 percent of its population living in cities. While fertility reductions often precipitate socioeconomic gains and vice versa, the process can clearly begin at very low socioeconomic levels.[30]

Moreover, from heavily Muslim Indonesia to heavily Catholic Central America, efforts to reduce fertility have prevailed despite daunting cultural and religious barriers to the empowerment of women and the acceptability of family planning. Nations with less successful or nonexistent population programs can learn from successful nations with similar cultural, religious, socioeconomic, and even geographic contexts.

★   ★   ★   ★

The challenge the world is facing with the population issue is both complex and demanding. At issue is whether we as a species can understand the consequences of continuing population growth and act quickly to slow it. Do we care enough about the world our children will live in to take action now? We regularly buy insurance to reduce uncertainty and to protect ourselves from future disasters, but there is no insurance policy that will pay greater dividends for the next generation than a modest investment in population stabilization today.

Above all, the world needs leadership on this issue. At the national level, the transition to low fertility rates requires strong leadership that deems population stabilization a priority. It also requires committed leaders who will speak openly about reproductive choices and the changing status of women, and who will put the building of schools, hiring of teachers, and distributing of condoms at the top of the list of national priorities. In light of the multiple economic, social, and environmental benefits of slowing population growth, the recent diversion of funding away from social services—including education and health care—in order to intensify military efforts in India, Iraq, Pakistan, and several Central African countries with burgeoning populations appears irresponsible.

Stabilizing population also depends on commitment from the international community. This year marks the fifth anniversary of the International Conference on Population and Development held in Cairo in 1994. The groundbreaking consensus reached then emphasized investments in people—including measures to increase access to and the quality of education and health care—as key to slowing population growth. A series of Cairo+5 events throughout the world will revisit the ideas and concerns voiced at that conference, while evaluating the progress made toward its program of action.[31]

While there has been limited progress toward many of Cairo's goals, there have been unacceptable failures. For instance, the 1994 conference concluded that providing quality reproductive health services to all those in need in developing nations would cost about $17 billion in the year 2000. By 2015, this would climb to $22 billion. The agreement was for donor countries to provide one third of the funds, with the developing countries providing the remaining two thirds.[32]

Unfortunately, industrial countries—and most important, the United States—have reneged on this commitment. In late 1998, the U.S. Congress withdrew all funding for the United Nations Population Fund, the primary source of international population assistance. The Cairo+5 meetings will provide an opportunity to call attention to nations who have broken their financial promises, as well as to focus on the other costs—for education, health care, job creation, and so on—that will continue to mount in the face of inaction.[33]

If we are facing a population emergency, it should be treated as such. It may be time for a campaign to convince couples everywhere to restrict their childbearing to replacement-level fertility—two children per women. In a recent book, *Maybe One: A Personal and Environmental Argument for Single-Child Families*, environmental writer Bill McKibben urges American couples to consider having only one child in order to slow population growth, lighten America's ecological footprint, and buy time to regain control of our environmental destiny. Zero Population Growth, a fast-growing U.S. nongovernmental organization, has long urged that couples limit the number of their surviving children to two. The time may have come for world leaders—the President of the United States, the Secretary-General of the United Nations, and the President of the World Bank, among others—to do the same.[34]

Given the potentially damaging consequences of continuing rapid population growth in countries that are struggling to provide the basic social services necessary to stabilize population and improve the welfare of their citizens, it may also be time to consider debt relief for some of these countries. The international debt of nations in sub-Saharan Africa—the global region with the least success in reducing population growth rates—stands at over 70 percent of the region's annual income.[35]

In late 1998, there were calls to relieve the debts of Central American nations heavily battered by Hurricane Mitch as well as nations in Africa devastated by AIDS. Debt relief is further justified to deal with the chronic emergencies created by lack of schooling, basic health care, and family planning. Debt relief for nations facing high fertility rates could help them get the brakes on population growth before they are overwhelmed by demographic fatigue.[36]

It may also be time for the world's wealthiest individuals, the 600 or so billionaires, to make a commitment to the global future as Ted Turner did in September 1997 when he pledged $1 billion to help the United Nations deal with problems such as population, environment, and health. It makes little sense for today's billionaires to argue that they will put their wealth in a foundation when they die, in perhaps 20 or 30 years, when the commitments are needed now to ensure that the world then is a livable one. The problems we are facing as a species are not unmanageable unless we permit them to become so.[37]

We live in a demographically divided world—one where some countries have reached or are approaching the stability of stage three of the demographic transition and one where rising mortality is forcing other countries back into stage one. Despite this sharpening contrast, our world is more environmentally integrated and more economically interdependent than ever before. In this integrated world, there are no longer "their problems" and "our problems." Only our problems.

Notes

CHAPTER 1. The Population Challenge

1. All population data in this paper, including per capita calculations, are from U.S. Bureau of the Census, *International Data
   Base*, electronic database, Suitland, MD, updated 30 November
   1998, and from United Nations, *World Population Prospects: The
   1998 Revision* (New York: December 1998) unless otherwise
   stated. We use Census data for the years 1950 to 1999 and U.N.
   data for the years 2000 to 2050. Although the two data sets do
   not differ substantially, Census provides annual data from 1950
   to 1999 while United Nations only provides data for every five
   years. However, the United Nations provides the latest projections to 2050, incorporating the most recent demographic sur-
   veys.
2. Fertility rates from United Nations, op. cit. note 1; moderation
   of past U.N. projections from Thomas Büettner, Population
   Division, Department of Economic and Social Affairs, United
   Nations, New York, discussion with Brian Halweil, 5 December
   1998.
3. Annual addition from Bureau of Census, op. cit. note 1; num-

ber of people coming of reproductive age from United Nations, op. cit. note 1.

4. Population growth rate from Bureau of Census, op. cit. note 1.

5. Population Reference Bureau, "1998 World Population Data Sheet," wall chart (Washington, DC: June 1998).

6. Ibid.

7. Thomas Robert Malthus, *An Essay on the Principle of Population (1798)*, from the Norton Critical Edition, ed. by Philip Appleman (New York: W.W. Norton & Company, 1976).

8. U.N. Food and Agriculture Organization (FAO), *Yearbook of Fishery Statistics: Catches and Landings* (Rome: various years); 1990–97 data from FAO, Rome, letters to Worldwatch, 11 November 1998; FAO, *The State of World Fisheries and Aquaculture* (Rome: 1997).

9. U.S. Department of Agriculture (USDA), *Production, Supply, and Distribution*, electronic database, Washington, DC, updated December 1998.

10. Ajay Khudania, "India Struggles with Fading Water Supply," *Hindustan Times*, 20 July 1998.

11. Fuelwood from FAO, *FAOSTAT Statistics Database*, <http://apps.fao.org>, viewed 5 July 1998; paper from International Institute for Environment and Development, *Towards a Sustainable Paper Cycle* (London: 1996), and from FAO, op. cit. this note; water from Sandra Postel, *Pillar of Sand* (New York: W.W. Norton & Company, in press); fossil fuels 1950–70 from United Nations, *World Energy Supplies 1950–74* (New York: 1976), and from United Nations, *Energy Statistics Yearbook* (New York: various years); fossil fuels 1970–95 from U.S. Department of Energy (DOE), Energy Information Administration (EIA), Office of Energy Markets and End Use, *International Statistics Database*, provided by Linda Doman at DOE, EIA, letter to Worldwatch, 5 August 1998; grain from USDA, op. cit. note 9.

12. Grain from USDA, op. cit. note 9; energy from DOE, op. cit. note 11.

13. USDA, op. cit. note 9.

14. Methodology and current fertility rate from United Nations, op. cit. note 1.

15. Büettner, op. cit. note 2.

CHAPTER 2. Grain Production

1. Figure 2–1 from U.S. Department of Agriculture (USDA), *Production, Supply, and Distribution (PS&D)*, electronic database, Washington, DC, updated December 1998; USDA, "World

Grain Database," unpublished printout, Washington, DC, 1991.

2. USDA, *PS&D*, op. cit. note 1; USDA, "World Grain Database," op. cit. note 1.

3. USDA, *PS&D*, op. cit. note 1; USDA, "World Grain Database," op. cit. note 1.

4. U.N. Food and Agriculture Organization (FAO), *FAOSTAT Statistics Database,* <http://apps.fao.org.>, viewed 5 August 1998.

5. Mark W. Rosegrant and Claudia Ringler, "World Food Markets into the 21st Century: Environmental and Resource Constraints and Policies," revision of a paper presented at the RIRDC-sponsored plenary session of the 41st Annual Conference of the Australian Agricultural and Resource Economics Society, Queensland, Australia, 22–25 January 1997; K.G. Soh and K.F. Isherwood, "Short Term Prospects for World Agriculture and Fertilizer Use," presentation at IFA Enlarged Council Meeting, International Fertilizer Industry Association, Monte Carlo, Monaco, 18–21 November 1997.

6. USDA, *PS&D*, op. cit. note 1.

7. Calculations based on current grain consumption per person in the United States and India from USDA, *PS&D*, op. cit. note 1.

8. USDA, *PS&D*, op. cit. note 1.

CHAPTER 3. Fresh Water

1. Tom Gardner-Outlaw and Robert Engelman, *Sustaining Water, Easing Scarcity (A Second Update)* (Washington, DC: Population Action International, 1997).

2. Colorado and Nile Rivers from Sandra Postel, *Pillar of Sand* (New York: W.W. Norton & Company, in press); Wang Chengshan, "What Does the Yellow River Tell?" *Openings,* Winter 1997.

3. David Seckler, David Molden, and Randolph Barker, "Water Scarcity in the Twenty-First Century" (Colombo, Sri Lanka: International Water Management Institute, 27 July 1998); Randolph E. Schmid, "Water Worry," *Associated Press,* 23 November 1998.

4. Peter Gleick, *The World's Water: 1998–1999* (Washington, DC: Island Press, 1998).

5. Figure of 1,000 tons of water for one ton of wheat from U.N. Food and Agriculture Organization (FAO), *Yield Response to Water* (Rome: 1979); "Water Scarcity as a Key Factor Behind Global Food Insecurity: Round Table Discussion," *Ambio,*

March 1998.

6. Nile flow from Sandra Postel, *Dividing the Waters: Food Security, Ecosystem Health, and the New Politics of Scarcity*, Worldwatch Paper 132 (Washington, DC: Worldwatch Institute, September 1996); U.S. Department of Agriculture, *Production, Supply, and Distribution*, electronic database, Washington, DC, updated December 1998.

7. Figure 3–1 from FAO, *FAOSTAT Statistics Database*, <http://apps. fao.org>, viewed 5 August 1998; Sandra Postel, "Water for Food Production: Will There Be Enough in 2025?" *BioScience*, August 1998.

8. Seckler, Molden, and Barker, op. cit. note 3.

CHAPTER 4. Biodiversity

1. Extinction rates from Chris Bright, *Life Out of Bounds* (New York: W.W. Norton & Company, 1998); species loss factors from John Tuxill and Chris Bright, "Losing Strands in the Web of Life," in Lester R. Brown et al., *State of the World 1998* (New York: W.W. Norton & Company, 1998).

2. Jonathan Baillie and Brian Groombridge, eds., *1996 IUCN Red List of Threatened Animals* (Gland, Switzerland: World Conservation Union–IUCN, 1996); Table 4–1 from Tuxill and Bright, op. cit. note 1.

3. Population concentration and migration estimates from Don Hinrichsen, *Coastal Waters of the World: Trends, Threats, and Strategies* (Washington, DC: Island Press, 1998); fisheries density from Peter Weber, "It Comes Down to the Coasts," *World Watch*, March/April 1994.

4. Global agricultural area from U.N. Food and Agriculture Organization (FAO), *Production Yearbook 1996* (Rome: 1997); Bangladesh from John Tuxill, "Appreciating the Benefits of Plant Biodiversity," in Lester R. Brown et al., *State of the World 1999* (New York: W.W. Norton & Company, 1999).

5. Tuxill, op. cit. note 4.

6. Ibid.

7. Extinction causes from Chris Bright, "Tracking the Ecology of Climate Change," in Lester R. Brown et al., *State of the World 1997* (New York: W.W. Norton & Company, 1997); impact of exotics from Bright, op. cit. note 1.

8. Peter M. Vitousek et al., "Human Alteration of the Global Nitrogen Cycle: Causes and Consequences," *Ecological Issues*, February 1997.

9. Ecological shift from Bright, op. cit. note 7.

CHAPTER 5. Energy

1. Figure 5-1 and discussion based on the following: energy use 1950–70 based on historic world oil, natural gas, hydroelectric, and coal use from United Nations, *World Energy Supplies 1950–74* (New York: 1976), and from United Nations, *Energy Statistics Yearbook* (New York: various years); energy use 1970–95 from U.S. Department of Energy (DOE), Energy Information Administration (EIA), Office of Energy Markets and End Use, *International Statistics Database*, provided by Linda Doman, DOE, EIA, e-mail to Worldwatch, 5 August 1998; energy use 1995–2020 interpolated based on figures for each five-year period from DOE, EIA, *International Energy Outlook 1998, April 1998* (Washington, DC: 1998); energy use 2020–2050 uses DOE's EIA figure for 2020 as the baseline year and growth rates for regional and global carbon emissions from 2020 to 2050 based on scenario IS92a in Robert T. Watson et al., eds., *Climate Change 1995: Impacts, Adaptations and Mitigation of Climate Change: Scientific-Technical Analyses: Contribution of Working Group II to the Second Assessment Report of the Intergovernmental Panel on Climate Change* (IPCC) (New York: Cambridge University Press, 1996).
2. Energy use 1995–2020 from DOE, *International Outlook*, op. cit. note 1; energy use 2020–2050 based on Watson et al., op. cit. note 1.
3. Energy use 1995–2020 from DOE, *International Outlook*, op. cit. note 1; energy use 2020–2050 based on Watson et al., op. cit. note 1.
4. Energy use 1995–2020 from DOE, *International Outlook*, op. cit. note 1; energy use 2020–2050 based on Watson et al., op. cit. note 1; energy reduction at lower population projection based on a output of 400 megawatts of electricity (or roughly 1 million tons of oil equivalent) for an average-sized coal-fired power plant, as per British Petroleum, *BP Statistical Review of World Energy 1998* (London: June 1998).
5. Energy use 1995–2020 from DOE, *International Outlook*, op. cit. note 1; energy use 2020–2050 based on Watson et al., op. cit. note 1.
6. Energy use 1995–2020 from DOE, *International Outlook*, op. cit. note 1; energy use 2020–2050 based on Watson et al., op. cit. note 1.
7. Energy use 1950–1970 from United Nations, *World Energy Supplies*, op. cit. note 1, and from United Nations, *Energy Yearbook*, op. cit. note 1; energy use 1970–95 from DOE, *Statistics*

Database, op. cit. note 1.

8. World oil production from United Nations, *World Energy Sup-plies,* op. cit. note 1, and from DOE, *Statistics Database,* op. cit. note 1; oil production projections from Jean Laherrere, Petro-consultants, Geneva, Switzerland, e-mail to Worldwatch, 12 July 1998; oil production projections from IPCC, provided by Jae Edmonds, e-mail to Worldwatch, 30 July 1998; Colin J. Campbell and Jean H. Laherrere, "The End of Cheap Oil," *Scientific American,* March 1998.

9. World Bank, *Rural Energy and Development: Improving Energy Supplies for Two Billion People* (Washington, DC: 1996); Rashmi Mayur and Bennett Daviss, "Tolls to Empower the World's Poorest People," *The Futurist,* October 1998.

CHAPTER 6. Oceanic Fish Catch

1. Figure 6–1 from U.N. Food and Agriculture Organization (FAO), *Yearbook of Fishery Statistics: Catches and Landings* (Rome: various years), with 1990–97 data from Maurizio Perotti, fishery statistician, Fishery Information, Data and Statistics Unit, Fisheries Department, FAO, Rome, letter to Worldwatch, 10 November 1998.

2. FAO, *The State of World Fisheries and Aquaculture, 1996* (Rome: 1997).

3. World's major fishing areas excludes inland catches and Antarctic waters. Eleven of 15 based on data from Perotti, op. cit. note 1; Atlantic cod from S.M. Garcia and C. Newton, "Current Situation, Trends, and Prospects in World Fisheries," in E.K. Pikitch, D.D. Huppert, and M.P. Sissenwine, *Global Trends: Fisheries Management,* American Fisheries Society (AFS) Symposium 20 (Bethesda, MD: AFS, 1997); bluefin tuna from Lisa Speer et al., *Hook, Line and Sinking: The Crisis in Marine Fisheries* (New York: Natural Resources Defense Council, February 1997).

4. FAO, op. cit. note 1.

5. Price of tuna from "Bluefin Tuna Reported on Brink of Extinction," *Journal of Commerce,* 11 October 1993.

6. Fisheries disputes from Johnathon Friedland, "Fish Stories These Days Are Tales of Deception and Growing Rivalry," *Wall Street Journal,* 25 November 1997; Greenpeace quote from William Branigin, "Global Accord Puts Curbs on Fishing," *Washington Post,* 4 August 1995.

7. American Sportfishing Association and Ocean Wildlife Campaign, "Slaughter at Sea," press release (Washington, DC: 12

January 1998); Dayton L. Alverson et al., *A Global Assessment of Fisheries Bycatch and Discards*, FAO Fisheries Technical Paper 339 (Rome: FAO, 1994).

8. Data for 1984–85 from FAO, *Aquaculture Production Statistics, 1984–1993*, FAO Fisheries Circular No. 815, Revision 7 (Rome: 1995); data for 1986–95 from FAO, *Aquaculture Production Statistics, 1986–1995*, FAO Fisheries Circular No. 815, Revision 9 (Rome: 1997); data for 1996–97 from Perotti, op. cit. note 1.

9. FAO, op. cit. note 1; 1990–97 data from Perotti, op. cit. note 1.

CHAPTER 7. Jobs

1. International Labour Organisation (ILO), *World Employment 1996/97* (Geneva: 1997), ILO, *Economically Active Population, 1950–2010* (Geneva: 1997); Michael Hopkins, "A Global Look at Jobless Growth, Poverty, and Unemployment: Trends and Future Prospects," prepared for ILO, September 1994; labor force projections are based on U.N. projections of population and dependency ratios and ILO projections of regional work activity rates for the year 2000.

2. Indermit S. Gill and Amit Dar, *Labor Market Policies and Interventions for Sustainable Employment Growth* (draft) (Washington, DC: World Bank, 7 September 1994).

3. Share of population under ages 25 and 15 from U.N. projections; ILO, "Labour Supply and Employment," *Spotlight* (newsletter of the Labour and Population Programme), December 1997.

4. ILO, *Jobs for Africa: A Policy Framework for an Employment-Intensive Growth Strategy* (Geneva: August 1997); poverty is defined here as surviving on less than $1 per person per day; labor force projections are based on U.N. projections of population and dependency ratios and ILO projections of regional work activity rates for the year 2000; additional background from ILO, op. cit. this note.

5. World Bank, *Claiming the Future: Choosing Prosperity in the Middle East and North Africa* (Washington, DC: 1995); unemployment data for Algeria from Roger Cohen, "In Algeria, Oil and Islam Make a Volatile Mixture," *New York Times*, 28 December 1996; growth in labor force from ILO, *Economically Active Population*, op. cit. note 1.

6. Labor force projections are based on U.N. projections of population and dependency ratios and ILO projections of regional work activity rates for the year 2000; Judy Pehrson, "Disgrun-

tled Chinese Worker Miss the 'Iron Rice Bowl'," *Christian Science Monitor*, 13 March 1998; Edmond Lococo, "China Feed, Livestock Mid-year Update," *Bridge News*, 30 June 1998; Associated Press, "China Fires 31/2 Million Government Employees," *San Francisco Examiner*, 10 August 1998; John Pomfret, "Workers and Reforms Fall into 'China's Slump'," *Washington Post*, 11 August 1998.

7. ILO, *World Employment 1996/97*, op. cit. note 1; youth unemployment rates from "Economic Indicators," *The Economist*, 22 August 1998.

8. Grainland data from U.S. Department of Agriculture, *Production, Supply, and Distribution*, electronic database, Washington, DC, updated December 1998; A.S. Oberai, *Population Growth, Employment and Poverty in Third-World Mega-Cities* (New York: St. Martin's Press, 1993).

9. Nancy Birdsall, "Government, Population, and Poverty: A Win-Win Tale," in Robert Cassen, ed., *Population and Development: Old Debates, New Conclusions* (New Brunswick, NJ: Transaction Publishers, 1994); Erik Eckholm, "China Jobless Fuel a Growth Industry," *New York Times*, 31 May 1998; Jeremy Rifkin and Robert L. Heilbroner, *The End of Work* (New York: Putnam, 1996); Steven Greenhouse, "The Relentless March of Labor's True Foe," *New York Times*, 2 August 1998; Herman E. Daly, "Population and Economic Globalization," *Organization & Environment*, December 1998.

CHAPTER 8. Infectious Diseases

1. Andrew Dobson, Mary S. Campbell, and Jensa Bell, "Fatal Synergisms: Interactions between Infectious Diseases, Human Population Growth, and Loss of Biodiversity," in Francesca Grifo and Joshua Rosenthal, eds., *Biodiversity and Human Health* (Washington, DC: Island Press, 1997); Table 8–1 from World Health Organization (WHO), *The World Health Report 1998* (Geneva: 1998), from Joint United Nations Programme on HIV/AIDS (UNAIDS) and WHO, *Report on Global HIV/AIDS Epidemic* (Geneva: June 1998), and from Jennifer Mallozi, "Tuberculosis: An Airborne Disease, *United Nations Chronicle*, spring 1998; the term "medium" is from A.J. McMichael, *Planetary Overload: Global Environmental Change and the Health of the Human Species* (New York: Cambridge University Press, 1993).

2. United Nations, *World Urbanization Prospects: 1996 Revision* (New York: 1997); David Pimentel et al., "Ecology of Increas-

ing Disease: Population Growth and Environmental Degradation," *Bioscience*, October 1998; Dobson, Campbell, and Bell, op. cit. note 1.

3. Dobson, Campbell, and Bell, op. cit. note 1; Centers for Disease Control, "Dengue/Dengue Hemorrhagic Fever: The Emergence of a Global Health Problem," *Emerging Infectious Diseases Dispatches*, April-June 1995.

4. United Nations Centre for Human Settlements (HABITAT), *An Urbanizing World: Global Report on Human Settlements, 1996* (Oxford, UK: Oxford University Press, 1996).

5. Pimentel et al., op. cit. note 2; Thomas Homer-Dixon and Valerie Percival, The Project on Environment, Population, and Security, *Environmental Scarcity and Violent Conflict: Briefing Book* (Washington, DC: American Association for the Advancement of Science, 1996); Peter Gleick, "The World's Water," *Issues in Science and Technology*, Summer 1998.

6. Wendy Marston, "In Peru's Shantytowns, Cholera Comes by the Bucket," *New York Times*, 8 December 1998; Anne E. Platt, *Infecting Ourselves: How Environmental and Social Disruptions Trigger Disease*, Worldwatch Paper 129 (Washington, DC: Worldwatch Institute, April 1996).

7. Pimentel et al., op. cit. note 2; Dr. Alfred Buck, School of Public Health, Johns Hopkins University, Baltimore, MD, discussion with Brian Halweil, 18 November 1998.

8. Platt, op. cit. note 6; Chiharu Kamimura, "Zimbabwean Activist Raps Government on AIDS," *Washington Times*, 13 November 1998.

9. "Cash, Please," *The Economist*, 5 September 1998; U.N. Development Programme, *Human Development Report 1998* (New York: Oxford University Press, 1998).

CHAPTER 9.   Cropland

1. Grain area from U.S. Department of Agriculture (USDA), *Production, Supply, and Distribution (PS&D)*, electronic database, Washington, DC, updated December 1998; USDA, "World Grain Database," unpublished printout, Washington, DC, 1991.

2. Faltering grain yields from Lester R. Brown, "Can We Raise Grain Yields Fast Enough?" *World Watch*, July/August 1997.

3. Figure 9–1 from USDA, *PS&D*, op, cit. note 1; 1950 grain area from USDA, "World Grain Database," op. cit. note 1.

4. Grain area from USDA, *PS&D*, op. cit. note 1.

5. Ibid; John Pomfret, "Congressional Aides Report High Hunger

Toll in North Korea," *Washington Post,* 20 August 1998.
6. USDA, *PS&D,* op. cit. note 1.
7. Erosion from Per Pinstrup Andersen and Rajul Pandya-Lorch, "Alleviating Poverty, Intensifying Agriculture, and Effectively Managing Natural Resources," Food, Agriculture, and the Environment Discussion Paper 1 (Washington, DC: International Food Policy Research Institute, 1994); fallow periods from Joy Tivy, *Agricultural Ecology* (Essex, UK: Longman Scientific and Technical, 1990).
8. Landlessness from United Nations, *Government Views on the Relationships between Population and Environment* (New York: United Nations, Department of Economic and Social Affairs, 1997).

CHAPTER 10. Forests

1. Table 10–1 based on population from U.S. Bureau of the Census, *International Data Base,* electronic database, Suitland, MD, updated 30 November 1998, and on forested area from Alan Durning, "Redesigning the Forest Economy," in Lester R. Brown et al., *State of the World 1994* (New York: W.W. Norton & Company, 1994).
2. Latin American deforestation factors from Paul Harrison, *The Third Revolution* (New York: Penguin Books, 1992); meat consumption from U.S. Department of Agriculture, *Production, Supply, and Distribution,* electronic database, Washington, DC, updated December 1998; world deforestation factors from Dirk Bryant, Daniel Nielsen, and Laura Tangley, *The Last Frontier Forests: Ecosystems and Economies on the Edge* (Washington, DC: World Resources Institute, 1997); fuelwood consumption to population growth correlation from U.N. Food and Agriculture Organization (FAO), *Regional Study on Wood Energy Today and Tomorrow in Asia* (Bangkok: 1997).
3. Paper and paperboard use from FAO, *FAOSTAT Statistics Database,* <http:// apps.fao.org.>, viewed 5 August 1998.
4. Current consumption from FAO, op. cit. note 3; projected consumption based on ibid.
5. Sustainable estimates and growth predictions from Duncan McLaren et al., *Tomorrow's World: Britain's Share in a Sustainable Future* (London: Earthscan Publications, 1998); McLaran's analysis is updated using FAO data for industrial roundwood for 1996.
6. Forest services from Norman Myers, "The World's Forests and Their Ecosystem Services," in Gretchen C. Daily, ed., *Nature's*

Services: Societal Dependence on Natural Ecosystems (Washington, DC: Island Press, 1997); carbon from deforestation from Richard A. Houghton, "Converting Terrestrial Ecosystems from Sources to Sinks of Carbon," *Ambio*, June 1996.

CHAPTER 11. Housing

1. United Nations Centre for Human Settlements (HABITAT), *An Urbanizing World: Global Report on Human Settlements, 1996* (Oxford, UK: Oxford University Press, 1996); Worldwatch housing projections are based on U.N. population projections and household size for 1995 from ibid., assuming a 15-percent reduction in number of people per household by 2050.
2. Table 11–1 contains Worldwatch housing projections as per note 1.
3. Worldwatch projections, as per note 1.
4. HABITAT, op. cit. note 1.
5. Ibid.; Erik Eckholm, "A Burst of Renewal Sweeps Old Beijing Into the Dumpsters," *New York Times*, 1 March 1998; Michael Janofsky, "Shortage of Housing for Poor Grows in US," *New York Times*, 28 April 1998.
6. Floor space per person from Gopal Ahluwalia, National Association of Home Builders, Washington, DC, discussion with Brian Halweil, 17 August 1998; HABITAT op. cit. note 1.
7. UNICEF, *The Progress of Nations* (New York: Oxford University Press, 1997); HABITAT, op. cit. note 1.
8. HABITAT, op. cit. note 1; Martin Brockerhoff and Ellen Brennan, "The Poverty of Cities in Developing Regions," *Population and Development Review*, March 1998; A.S. Oberai, *Population Growth, Employment and Poverty in Third-World Mega-Cities* (New York: St. Martin's Press, 1993).

CHAPTER 12. Climate Change

1. Figure 12–1, for 1950–95, from G. Marland et al., "Global, Regional, and National CO_2 Emission Estimates from Fossil Fuel Burning, Cement Production, and Gas Flaring: 1751–1995 (revised January 9, 1998)," Oak Ridge National Laboratory, <http://cdiac.esd.ornl.gov/>, viewed 14 August 1998; atmospheric carbon dioxide levels from C. D. Keeling and T. P. Whorf, "Atmospheric CO_2 Concentrations (ppmv) Derived from In Situ Air Samples Collected at Mauna Loa Observatory, Hawaii, 1958–1997 (revised August 1998),"

Scripps Institute of Oceanography, <http://cdiac.esd.
ornl.gov/>, viewed 14 August 1998; Figure 12–2 from James
Hansen et al., Goddard Institute for Space Studies, Surface Air
Temperature Analyses, "Global Land-Ocean Temperature
Index," <http://www.giss.nasa.gov/Data/GISTEMP>, viewed
14 December 1998.

2. Carbon emissions 1995–2020 interpolated based on figures for
each five-year period from U.S. Department of Energy (DOE),
Energy Information Administration (EIA), *International Energy
Outlook 1998, April 1998* (Washington, DC: 1998); carbon
emissions 2020–50 use DOE's EIA figure for 2020 as the baseline year and growth rates for regional and global carbon emissions from 2020 to 2050 based on scenario IS92a in Robert T.
Watson et al., eds., *Climate Change 1995: Impacts, Adaptations
and Mitigation of Climate Change: Scientific-Technical Analyses:
Contribution of Working Group II to the Second Assessment Report
of the Intergovernmental Panel on Climate Change* (IPCC) (New
York: Cambridge University Press, 1996); J.T. Houghton et al.,
"Stabilization of Atmospheric Greenhouse Gases: Physical,
Biological and Socio-economic Implications," technical paper
of the IPCC, February 1997.

3. Carbon emissions 1995–2020 from DOE, op. cit. note 2; carbon emissions 2020–50 based on Watson et al., op. cit. note 2.

4. Carbon emissions 1950–1995 from Marland et al., op. cit. note
1; carbon emissions 1995–2020 from DOE, op. cit. note 2; carbon emissions 2020–50 based on Watson et al., op. cit. note 2.

5. Carbon emissions 1995–2020 from DOE, op. cit. note 2; carbon emissions 2020–50 based on Watson et al., op. cit. note 2.

6. Marland et al., op. cit. note 1; carbon emissions 1995–2020
from DOE, op. cit. note 2; carbon emissions 2020–50 based on
Watson et al., op. cit. note 2.

7. Sandra Brown et al., "Management of Forests for Mitigation of
Greenhouse Gas Emissions," in Watson et al., op. cit. note 2;
Richard A. Houghton, "Converting Terrestrial Ecosystems
from Sources to Sinks of Carbon," *Ambio*, June 1996; carbon
from Asian fires from Sander Thoenes, "In Asia's Big Haze,
Man Battles Man-Made Disaster," *Christian Science Monitor*, 28
October 1997.

CHAPTER 13. Materials

1. Materials use from United States Geological Survey (USGS),
Mineral Yearbook and Mineral Commodity Summaries (Reston,

VA: various years), from data supplied by Grecia Matos, Minerals and Materials Analysis Section, USGS, Reston, VA, 27 July 1998, from Great Britain Overseas Geological Survey, *Statistical Survey of the Mineral Industry* (London: various years), from United Nations, *Industrial Commodity Statistics Yearbook* (New York: various years), and from U.N. Food and Agriculture Organization, *FAOSTAT Statistics Database,* <http://apps.fao.org.>, viewed 15 June 1998.

2. United Nations Development Programme, *Human Development Report 1998* (New York: Oxford University Press, 1998).

3. U.S. construction materials from USGS, op. cit. note 1; Asian infrastructure from Asian Development Bank, *Emerging Asia: Changes and Challenges* (Manila: 1997).

4. Cement based on data from Henrik van Oss, Cement Commodity Specialist, USGS, Reston, VA, discussion with Payal Sampat, Worldwatch Institute, 6 November 1998, from Henrik G. van Oss, "Cement," in USGS, *Mineral Yearbook 1996* (Reston, VA: 1996), and from Seth Dunn, "Carbon Emissions Resume Rise," in Lester R. Brown, Michael Renner, and Christopher Flavin, *Vital Signs 1998* (New York: W.W. Norton & Company, 1998). If carbon emissions from fuel combustion and calcination are combined, cement production contributed some 300 million tons of carbon in 1995, approximately 5 percent of global emissions that year; this total does not include electricity used by cement producers. Leaching and methane emissions from landfills and U.S. methane emissions from U.S. Department of Energy, *Annual Energy Review* database, <http://tonto.eia.doe.gov/aer/>, viewed 5 October 1998.

5. Ore grades from Nathan Rosenberg, "Technology," in Glenn Porter, ed., *Encyclopedia of American Economic History: Studies of Principal Movements and Ideas,* vol. 1 (New York: Charles Scribner's Sons, 1980), and from Daniel Edelstein, copper commodity specialist, USGS, Reston, VA, discussion with Payal Sampat, Worldwatch Institute, 6 October 1998; species extinctions from Edward O. Wilson, *The Diversity Of Life* (New York: W.W. Norton & Company, 1992).

6. Figure 13–1 from USGS and other sources cited in note 1, with projections based on materials data in USGS, op. cit. note 1, and on population data from United Nations, *World Population Prospects: The 1998 Revision* (New York: December 1998).

7. Mining shift to Latin America from Payal Sampat, "Metals Exploration Explodes in the South," in Brown, Renner, and Flavin, op. cit. note 4.

CHAPTER 14. Urbanization

1. Table 14–1 calculated by applying the share of world population that is urban from United Nations, *World Urbanization Prospects: 1996 Revision* (New York: 1997) to the latest United Nations population projections; U.N. projections for share of world population that is urban only go to 2030, so figures for 2040–50 are Worldwatch extrapolations.
2. London figure from Andrew Lees, *Cities Perceived: Urban Society in European and American Thought: 1820–1940* (New York: Columbia University Press, 1985); United Nations, op. cit. note 1.
3. United Nations, op. cit. note 1.
4. Ibid.
5. Martin Brockerhoff and Ellen Brennan, "The Poverty of Cities in Developing Regions," *Population and Development Review*, March 1998.

CHAPTER 15. Protected Natural Areas

1. World Conservation Union–IUCN, *Protected Areas and Demographic Change: Planning for the Future*, proceedings of the IVth World Congress on National Parks and Protected Areas, Caracas, Venezuela, 10–21 February 1992 (Gland, Switzerland: 1992).
2. Sunil Sampat, Bombay, India, e-mail to Brian Halweil, 15 May 1998; Juan Manuel Martinez Valdez, ECOPOL (Ecologia y Poblacion), Mexico City, discussion with Brian Halweil, 10 May 1998; IUCN, "Las Areas Naturales Protegidas de la Argentina" (Buenos Aries, January 1998); Table 15–1 from A. de Sherbinin, *Population Dynamics and Protected Areas: Options for Action*, IUCN Issues in Social Policy (Gland, Switzerland: forthcoming), from Ministry of Tourism and Civil Aviation, Department of Tourism, *Annual Statistical Report 1996* (Kathmandu, Nepal: 1996), from Alan Mairson, "The Everglades: Dying for Help," *National Geographic*, April 1994, from Kevin Collins, National Parks and Conservation Association, discussion with Brian Halweil, 29 April 1998, from "Recreational Golf in the US," *Christian Science Monitor*, 9 April 1998, from Edwin Moure, Biscayne National Park, Florida, discussion with Brian Halweil, 2 August 1998, and from "Sugar's Latest Everglades Threat," *New York Times*, 29 April 1998.
3. Stan Stevens, "The Legacy of Yellowstone," in Stan Stevens,

ed., *Conservation Through Cultural Survival: Indigenous People and Protected Areas* (Washington, DC: Island Press, 1997).

4. De Sherbinin, op. cit. note 2.

5. Ibid.

6. Collins, op. cit. note 2; "Sugar's Latest Everglades Threat," op. cit. note 2.

7. Don Hinrichsen, *Coastal Waters of the World: Trends, Threats, and Strategies* (Washington, DC: Island Press, 1998).

8. Farah Vakil, Bombay Environmental Action Group, Bombay, India, e-mail to Brian Halweil, 4 May 1998; Betty Spence, "Getting Along With the Elephants," *Christian Science Monitor*, 11 February 1998; James C. McKinley Jr., "It's Kenya's Farmers vs. Wildlife, and the Animals are Losing," *New York Times*, 2 August 1998.

9. Douglas Martin, "On City's Playing Fields, a Turf War," *New York Times,*, 5 April 1998; United Nations, *World Urbanization Prospects: 1996 Revision* (New York: 1997); U.S. National Park Service, <http://www.nps.gov/planning/yosemite/vip/fact/f01.htm>; Tom Kenworthy, "The Cost of the Wild," *Washington Post*, 10 August 1997; "Congress Moving to Extend Park Fees, Despite Protests," *Washington Post*, 10 August 1998.

Chapter 16. Education

1. Figure 16–1 based on United Nations, *World Population Prospects: The 1998 Revision* (New York: December 1998).

2. Ibid.

3. Current student-teacher ratio is an average taken from U.N. Development Programme (UNDP), *Human Development Report 1996* (New York: Oxford University Press, 1996), which uses data from 1992; African education statistics from Fay Chung, "Education in Africa Today," in Jacques Delor, *Learning: the Treasure Within*, report to UNESCO of the International Commission on Education for the Twenty-First Century (Paris: UNESCO, 1996).

4. Illiterate adults from UNESCO, *World Education Report 1998: Teachers and Teaching in a Changing World* (Paris: 1998); chronically hungry from U.N. Food and Agriculture Organization, *The Sixth World Food Survey* (Rome: 1997); people without access to a decent toilet from UNICEF, *The Progress of Nations* (New York: Oxford University Press, 1997).

5. UNESCO benchmark from Delor, op. cit. note 3; education investment from UNDP, op. cit. note 3.

6. Delor, op. cit. note 3.

Chapter 17. Waste

1. Waste volume estimates from William Rathje and Cullen Murphy, *Rubbish! The Archaeology of Garbage* (New York: Harper Collins, 1992); international waste production data from International Maritime Organization (IMO), *Global Waste Survey Final Report* (London: 1995); Table 17–1 based on the following: average municipal solid waste generation rates from U.S. Environmental Protection Agency, *Characterization of Municipal Solid Waste* (Washington, DC: 1995), and from Roger Pfammeter and Roland Schertenleib, "Non-Governmental Refuse Collection in Low-Income Urban Areas," SANDEC Report No. 1/96 (Duebenborf, Switzerland: Swiss Federal Institute for Environmental Science and Technology, Department of Water and Sanitation in Developing Countries, March 1996); volume of plastic from Rathje and Murphy, op. cit. this note; IMO data from IMO, op. cit. this note; sanitation from World Health Organization (WHO), Water Supply and Sanitation Collaborative Council, and UNICEF, *Water Supply and Sanitation Sector Monitoring Report, 1996* (New York: WHO, 1996), and from UNICEF, *The Progress of Nations* (New York: Oxford University Press, 1997).

2. Waste production data and correlation to economic level from Organisation for Economic Co-operation and Development (OECD), *OECD Environmental Data 1995* (Paris: 1995), and from Pfammeter and Schertenleib, op. cit. note 1. OECD lists municipal waste per capita for member countries as 500 kilos per person for 1992. Using updated population figures, we calculate per capita generation to be some 442 kilos per person in 1990. Data for developing countries are scarce, but using the commonly cited figure of half a kilo per person per day, their citizens would generate 183 kilos per year.

3. Access to sanitation from WHO, Water Supply and Sanitation Collaborative Council, and UNICEF, op. cit. note 1 (based on a survey of 84 of 130 developing countries, not including Eastern Europe or Central Asia), and from UNICEF, op. cit. note 1; disease incidence from WHO, "Water and Sanitation," Fact Sheet No. 112 (Geneva: November 1996); diarrhea mortality from UNICEF, op. cit. note 1.

4. Rural sanitation shortage and future sanitation requirements from WHO, Water Supply and Sanitation Collaborative Council, and UNICEF, op. cit. note 1; urban sanitation impacts from UNICEF, op. cit. note 1; 3 billion is a Worldwatch estimate based on United Nations, *World Urbanization Prospects: 1996*

Revision (New York: 1997).

5. Statistics from WHO, Water Supply and Sanitation Collaborative Council, and UNICEF, op. cit. note 1.

CHAPTER 18. Conflict

1. As per a definition provided by Joan M. Nelson in a report prepared for the Rockefeller Brothers Fund, Project on World Security, "Poverty, Inequality, and Conflict in Developing Countries," 1998, conflict here refers to intrastate conflicts among groups, or between one or more groups and the state. International conflicts are also considered, though it is acknowledged that, in the context of population-related resource scarcity, international conflicts are relatively rare (though there may be international repercussions of intrastate conflicts). Individual violence, including crime and domestic violence, is not the main focus here. Gunther Baechler, "Why Environmental Transformation Causes Violence: A Synthesis," *Environmental Change and Security Project Report*, Woodrow Wilson Center, Issue 4, Spring 1998; Thomas Homer-Dixon and Valerie Percival, The Project on Environment, Population, and Security, *Environmental Scarcity and Violent Conflict: Briefing Book* (Washington, DC: American Association for the Advancement of Science, 1996).

2. Baechler, op. cit. note 1; Table 18–1 based on Homer-Dixon and Percival, op. cit. note 1, and on John Pomfret, "With Its Mighty Rivers Drying Up, China Faces Dire Water Shortage," *Washington Post*, 25 October 1998.

3. Thomas Homer-Dixon, "Environmental Scarcity and Intergroup Conflict," in Michael T. Klare and Daniel C. Thomas, eds., *World Security: Challenges for a New Century* (New York: St. Martin's Press, 1994); Homer-Dixon and Percival, op. cit. note 1.

4. Homer-Dixon, op. cit. note 3; Rockefeller Brothers Fund, op. cit. note 1; Robert Mandel, *Conflict Over the World's Resources* (New York: Greenwood Press, 1988).

5. Frances Moore Lappe et al., *World Hunger: 12 Myths* (New York: Grove Press, 1998).

6. Kimberly Kelly and Thomas Homer-Dixon, The Project on Environment, Population, and Security, *Environmental Scarcity and Violent Conflict: The Case of Gaza* (Washington, DC: American Association for the Advancement of Science, 1996); Sandra Postel, *Pillar of Sand* (New York: W.W. Norton & Company, in press); John Waterbury and Dale Whittington, "Playing

Chicken on the Nile? The Implication of Microdam Development in the Ethiopian Highlands and Egypt's New Valley Project," *Natural Resources Forum*, August 1998.

7. Ovais Subhani, "Army Courts To Quell Karachi Violence," *Reuters*, 20 November 1998; Peter Gizewski and Thomas Homer-Dixon, The Project on Environment, Population, and Security, *Environmental Scarcity and Violent Conflict: The Case of Pakistan* (Washington, DC: American Association for the Advancement of Science, 1996); Peter Gizewski and Thomas Homer-Dixon, The Project on Environment, Population, and Security, *Urban Growth and Violence: Will the Future Resemble the Past?* (Washington, DC: American Association for the Advancement of Science, 1995).

8. Thomas F. Homer-Dixon, *Environment, Scarcity, and Violence* (forthcoming; submitted to Princeton University Press).

CHAPTER 19. Meat Production

1. Figure 19–1 from FAO, *1948–1985 World Crop and Livestock Statistics* (Rome: 1987), from FAO, *FAO Production Yearbooks 1988–1991* (Rome: 1990–93), and from U.S. Department of Agriculture (USDA), Foreign Agricultural Service, *Livestock and Poultry: World Markets and Trade*, October 1998.

2. FAO, *Crop and Livestock Statistics*, op. cit. note 1; FAO, *Production Yearbooks*, op. cit. note 1; USDA, op. cit. note 1.

3. FAO, *Crop and Livestock Statistics*, op. cit. note 1; FAO, *Production Yearbooks*, op. cit. note 1; USDA, op. cit. note 1; grain-to-poultry ratio derived from Robert V. Bishop et al., *The World Poultry Market—Government Intervention and Multilateral Policy Reform* (Washington, DC: USDA, 1990); grain-to-pork ratio from Leland Southard, Livestock and Poultry Situation and Outlook Staff, Economic Research Service (ERS), USDA, Washington, DC, discussion with Worldwatch, 27 April 1992; grain-to-beef ratio based on Allen Baker, Feed Situation and Outlook Staff, ERS, USDA, Washington, DC, discussion with Worldwatch, 27 April 1992.

4. USDA, *Production, Supply, and Distribution*, electronic database, Washington, DC, updated December 1998.

5. Ibid.

6. Ibid.

7. Ibid.; idled land from USDA, ERS, "AREI Updates: Cropland Use in 1997," No. 5 (Washington, DC: 1997).

CHAPTER 20. Income

1. Gross world product data from Worldwatch update of Angus Maddison, *Monitoring the World Economy 1820–1992* (Paris: Organisation for Economic Co-operation and Development, 1995), and of International Monetary Fund (IMF), *World Economic Outlook*, October 1998 (Washington, DC: 1998); Herbert R. Block, *The Planetary Product in 1980: A Creative Pause?* (Washington, DC: U.S. Department of State, 1981).
2. Figure 20–1 from Worldwatch update of Maddison, op. cit. note 1, and IMF, op. cit. note 1.
3. IMF, op. cit. note 1.
4. Rodolfo A. Bulatao, *The Value of Family Planning Programs in Developing Countries* (Santa Monica, CA: RAND, 1998).
5. IMF, op. cit. note 1.
6. World Bank, *Global Development Finance, 1998* (Washington, DC: 1998).
7. World Bank, *Food Security for the World*, statement prepared for the World Food Summit by the World Bank, 12 November 1996.
8. Fuelwood from U.N. Food and Agriculture Organization (FAO), *FAOSTAT Statistics Database*, <http://apps.fao.org>, viewed 5 July 1998; paper ibid. and from International Institute for Environment and Development, *Towards a Sustainable Paper Cycle* (London: 1996); fish catch from FAO, *Yearbook of Fishery Statistics: Catches and Landings* (Rome: various years), with 1990–97 data from Maurizio Perotti, fishery statistician, Fishery Information, Data and Statistics Service, Fisheries Department, FAO, Rome, letter to Worldwatch, 10 November 1998; grain from U.S. Department of Agriculture, *Production, Supply, and Distribution*, electronic database, Washington, DC, updated December 1998; fossil fuels 1950–70 from United Nations, *World Energy Supplies 1950–74* (New York: 1976), and from United Nations, *Energy Statistics Yearbook* (New York: various years); fossil fuels 1970–95 from U.S. Department of Energy (DOE), Energy Information Administration (EIA), Office of Energy Markets and End Use, *International Statistics Database*, provided by Linda Doman, DOE, EIA, e-mail to Worldwatch, 5 August 1998.

CHAPTER 21. The Emergence of Demographic Fatigue

1. Frank Notestein, "Population—The Long View," in P.W. Schultz, ed., *Food for The World* (University of Chicago Press:

1945); Warren Thompson, "Population," *American Journal of Sociology*, vol. 34, no. 6 (1929).

2. Table 21–1 from Population Reference Bureau (PRB), "1998 World Population Data Sheet," wall chart (Washington DC: June 1998).

3. Figure 21–1 from U.S. Department of Agriculture (USDA), *Production, Supply, and Distribution*, electronic database, Washington, DC, updated December 1998.

4. Mark W. Rosegrant and Claudia Ringler, "World Food Markets into the 21st Century: Environmental and Resource Constraints and Policies," revision of a paper presented at the RIRDC-sponsored plenary session of the 41st Annual Conference of the Australian Agricultural and Resource Economics Society, Queensland, Australia, 22–25 January 1997.

5. Population Action International, *Global Freshwater Resources* (Washington, DC: 1997).

6. Rodolfo A. Bulatao, *The Value of Family Planning Programs in Developing Countries* (Santa Monica, CA: RAND, 1998).

7. Joint United Nations Programme on HIV/AIDS (UNAIDS) and World Health Organization (WHO), *Report on the Global HIV/AIDS Epidemic* (Geneva: June 1998); U.S. Bureau of Census, *International Data Base*, electronic database, Suitland, MD, updated 30 November 1998.

8. Life expectancy estimates from United Nations, *World Population Prospects: The 1998 Revision* (New York: December 1998).

9. UNAIDS and WHO, op. cit. note 7.

10. Ibid.

11. Table 21–3 based on the following: Jared Diamond, *Guns, Germs, and Steel: The Fates of Human Societies* (New York: W.W. Norton & Company, 1997); Joshua Lederberg et al, *Emerging Infections: Microbial Threats to Health in the United States* (Washington, DC: National Academy Press, 1992); Johnthan Mann and Daniel Tarantola, eds., *AIDS in the World II* (New York: Oxford University Press, 1996). The HIV/AIDS pandemic also differs substantially from past plagues in the disease gestation period. While the Black Death, smallpox, and influenza all had short gestations typical of global plagues, with victims succumbing within days or weeks of infection, HIV/AIDS has an unusually long gestation. Adults typically die within 5–10 years of HIV infection, though costly antiretroviral therapies can extend lifespans; children generally die within 6 months to 2 years of infection. The lengthened gestation leads to a slow-steady growth pattern, rather than a boom-bust, as with other plagues, complicating responsive public health measures and making the disease particularly insidious.

12. USDA, op. cit. note 3.
13. David Seckler, David Molden, and Randolph Barker, "Water Scarcity in the Twenty-First Century" (Colombo, Sri Lanka: International Water Management Institute, 27 July 1998).
14. Ibid.
15. USDA, op. cit. note 3.
16. Valerie Percival and Thomas Homer-Dixon, The Project on Environment, Population, and Security, *Environmental Scarcity and Violent Conflict: The Case of Rwanda* (Washington, DC: American Association for the Advancement of Science, 1995).
17. Sandra Postel, *Pillar of Sand* (New York: W.W. Norton, in press).
18. Ibid.
19. PRB, op. cit. note 2.
20. Herman E. Daly, "Population and Economic Globalization," *Organization & Environment*, December 1998.
21. Craig Lasher, "U.S. Population Policy Since the Cairo Conference," *Environmental Change and Security Project Report*, The Woodrow Wilson Center, spring 1998.
22. Population trajectories from United Nations. op. cit. note 8.
23. Thomas R. Sinclair, "Limits to Crop Yield?" in American Society of Agronomy, Crop Science Society of America, and Soil Science Society of America, *Physiology and Determination of Crop Yield* (Madison, WI: 1994).
24. USDA, op. cit. note 3.
25. Edward O. Wilson, *The Diversity of Life* (New York: W.W. Norton & Company, 1993).
26. Nancy E. Riley, "Gender, Power, and Population Change," *Population Bulletin*, May 1997.
27. Barbara Barnett (with Jane Stein), *Women's Voices, Women's Lives: The Impact of Family Planning* (Research Triangle Park, NC: Family Health International, 1998).
28. Infant mortality from United Nations, op. cit. note 8.
29. Bulatao, op. cit. note 6.
30. Ibid.
31. Adriana Gomez, "Five Years After ICPD: The Challenge of Cairo Continues," *Women's Health Journal*, February 1998.
32. "Broken Promises: U.S. Public Funding for International and Domestic Reproductive Health Care" (draft), prepared by the Mobilizing Resources Task Force, U.S. NGOs in Support of the Cairo Consensus, Washington, DC, 15 July 1998.
33. Ibid.; United Nations Population Fund, "Executive Director's Statement on the Withdrawal of U.S. Funding from UNFPA," New York, 20 October 1998.
34. Bill McKibben, *Maybe One* (New York: Simon & Schuster, 1998).

35. World Bank, *Global Development Finance*, electronic database, Washington, DC, updated 1998.
36. EURODAD, "Eurodad and Central American NGOs launch International Call for Action," press release, 5 November 1998.
37. Forbes, "1998 World's Richest People," <http://www.forbes.com>; David Rhode, "Ted Turner Plans a $1 Billion Gift for U.N. Agencies," *New York Times*, 19 November 1997.

Index

ABOUT THE AUTHORS

LESTER R. BROWN is founder, president, and a senior researcher at the Worldwatch Institute. The senior author of the Institute's two annuals, *State of the World* and *Vital Signs,* he is perhaps best known for his pioneering work on the concept of environmentally sustainable development.

GARY GARDNER is a senior researcher at the Institute and has written on agriculture, waste, and materials issues for the annual *State of the World* report, *World Watch* magazine, and other Institute publications.

BRIAN HALWEIL is a staff researcher and writes on issues related to food and agriculture, HIV/AIDS, cigarettes, and biotechnology.